Dedication

This book is dedicated
to the members of
the Sierra Club, Greenpeace,
the Audubon Society,
and to those who seek to live
in harmony with
our fellow creatures.

"Cooling it" on the trail

Hiking Kauai

The Garden Isle

by Robert Smith

A Hawaiian Outdoors Adventures Publication

First edition 1977
Second edition 1979
Third edition 1983
Fourth printing 1987
Fourth edition 1989
Fifth edition 1996
Sixth edition 1999
Seventh edition 2002

Copyright 1977, 1979, 1983, 1989,
          1996, 1999, 2002 by Robert Smith

Layout by N. Karakawa

Photos by Robert Smith

Cover photo: Kilohana Lookout at the end of the Alakai
Swamp Trail overlooking Wainiha Valley and Hanalei Bay.

Library of Congress Card Catalog
          83-60684
Int'l Standard Book Number
          0-924308-09-5
Manufactured in the United States
Published by
          Hawaiian Outdoor Adventures
          Publications
          34 Kaui Place
          Kula, Maui, Hawaii 96790

Acknowledgments

I am in indebted to number of people who generously offered their time and effort to make this book possible. Ralph E. Daehler, District Forester, (Retired) for the State of Hawaii and Mac Hori, Park Supervisor (Retired) at Kokee State Park, contributed their knowledge and the resources of their respective departments. I am particularly grateful for their patience and good humor in response to my queries and requests. A very special "mahalo" to Roy Fujioka for sharing his knowledge of the island and to Carol, Francis, and Mac Fujioka for their generosity. Lastly, many thanks to Norbert Karakawa for his computer skills and advice in designing this edition.

Robert Smith
Kula, Maui, Hawaii

Books by Robert Smith

Hawaii's Best Hiking Trails
Hiking Maui, the Valley Isle
Hiking Oahu, the Capital Isle
Hiking Hawaii, the Big Island
Hiking Kauai, the Garden Isle

Video by Robert Smith

Hawaii On Foot

CONTENTS

Pick your own

Part I: Introduction

Waimea Canyon: "The Grand Canyon of the Pacific"

The Island

Kauai offers more natural beauty than most people can absorb. Island trails lead to magnificent waterfalls, to breathtaking vistas into Kauai's canyonlands and to the wilderness area along the Na Pali Coast. No one I have ever known has been disappointed by this enchanted land.

Some people call the island Kauai-a-mano-ka-lani-po — "The fountainhead of many waters from on high and bubbling up from below." Others regard it as "The Grand Canyon of the Pacific" or "The Garden Island" and still others say it is "The land of the Menehune." But even if you just call it "Kauai" — time of plenty, or fruitful season — it is still a land of beauty, grandeur and adventure, and a challenge to the outdoorsperson.

Kauai lays claim to a number of firsts and unique characteristics. It is the oldest island in the Hawaiian Islands, it is the northernmost inhabited island in the chain, and it was the first one visited by Captain Cook — though that is a rather dubious distinction. Still other things of local pride include Mt. Waialeale, the wettest spot on earth; the only place on earth where the iliau, a rare and unique plant, is to be found; and the home of the legendary Menehune, a race of pygmies who were short, industrious, strong, and highly skilled workers in stone.

Not unlike the neighboring islands, tourism on Kauai with its 58,000-plus inhabitants has grown as has the number of people taking to the island's trails. Kauai lies 102 air miles northwest of Honolulu — about a 20-minute flight. Most visitors to Kauai are seeking its solitude and slower pace of life, and many find these in the verdant valleys of the remote Na Pali coast and in the lush canyon lands of Waimea. Conveniently, the State of Hawaii and the County of Kauai have established miles of trails and jeep roads into remote areas which will reveal some of the island's secrets.

There is a lot of hiking pleasure packed into this almost circular little island of 555 square miles. But it is important to remember that natural and man-made forces have had and continue to have a dramatic impact on Kauai's topography. Hurricanes, 400-plus inches of rain in several places, the influx of new residents, and the increasing numbers of visitors affect trail conditions. A trail that was cleared and brushed and in good condition can become overgrown after a few weeks of heavy rain, particularly if it is not heavily traveled. For example, the trails in the Kokee/Waimea area are maintained by government and volunteer groups. However, 200-500 inches of rain annually in that area impacts greatly on trail conditions so that the description in this book may differ a bit from what you experience.

In addition to damage to trails caused by natural forces, some people destroy or remove trailhead signs, trail markers and trail mileage posts for some inexplicable reason. Consequently, I have provided clear directions to trailheads   and trail descriptions that do not rely on posted trail markers.

Getting around Kauai has been made easier since 1992, when Kauai inaugurated a public bus system that runs from Hanalei to Kekaha. Call (808) 241-6410 for information and routes. Rental vehicles are available from Lihue Airport.

At present, hitchhiking is legal, but **DO NOT HITCHHIKE ALONE.**

Luxury camping - Kokee State Park

Safe Hiking in Hawaii

The State Department of Health has issued a warning to campers and hikers that portable water filters may protect against giardia, salmonella and other bacteria and parasites, but they do not protect from the dangerous bacterium leptospirosis. Health officials say that only boiling or chemical treatment will control this disease that is found in surface water throughout Hawaii. It enters the body through breaks in the skin or through mucous membranes and can cause flu-like symptoms. The disease can also be fatal. Recently, some manufacturers of water devices claim that their filters do filter out leptospirosis. Carefully examine their evidence and research before purchasing their product. Drinking water is available from streams in many areas, but should be boiled or treated, since cattle, pigs, rats and goats may share the water supply. To avoid the chance of illness, carry at least one quart of water per person.

Hiking and backpacking have increased in popularity in recent years in Hawaii, not only because they are inexpensive ways to travel but also because they are different ways to experience a place. In Hawaii, outdoor experiences are outstanding; however, the outdoorsperson should be

aware of a number of problems. For one, violent
actions against hikers and campers, while
remaining low in percentage considering the
numbers who are taking to the trail, have
increased. As any community grows and urban
centers develop, the ills of city life, including vio-
lence and crime, follow. Consequently, hikers particularly females are cautioned never to hike or
camp alone. As a general rule, the farther you
hike and camp away from populated areas, the
safer your experience is likely to be. NEVER leave
valuables unprotected. I always carry a daypack
or waistpack containing those items which I can-
not afford to lose — wallet, airline ticket, camera
— and I carry it everywhere.

Another problem facing the hiker in Hawaii is
the lack of trailhead signs and trailhead markers.
Most of the trails contained in this book are well-
defined, but some are not marked. Consequently,
I provide detailed directions to the trailhead and
a trail narrative that makes the trail easy to follow. I have included a wide selection of trips from
short, easy family walks to long, difficult hikes
and backpacks. All of the trails are on public lands
so that no permission is needed to hike. I have
included hikes on private land in past editions of
this book, but no longer do so since landowners
will not grant permission to enter their lands.

Hikers and campers are always relieved to
learn that there are no poisonous snakes in
Hawaii. Poisonous centipedes and scorpions are
found at low elevations, however. The two biggest
pests in Hawaii are the mosquito and the cock-

roach. Both are troublesome and they can make an outdoor experience disagreeable unless precautions are taken. You will have to live with the cockroach, but all of the mosquito lotions and sprays seem to provide effective protection. Because of the wet climate, be prepared to make frequent applications.

Sadly, too many hikers annually have lost their lives or are injured because they have violated time-tested safety rules. Remember,

1. **DO NOT HIKE ALONE.**
2. **DO NOT HIKE OFF THE TRAIL**.
3. Leave your route and expected time of return with a reliable person.
4. Carry water, snacks, mirror, flashlight, waterproof matches and a whistle. Extra water should not be regarded as a burden.
5. Wear bright clothing.
6. Wear appropriate clothing and hiking boots or strong shoes.
7. If lost, find an open area and stay put.
8. Carry first-aid supplies.
9. During heavy rain, go to high ground. Flash flooding is common in Hawaii.
10. Darkness sets in right after sunset.

To protect the environment, remember,
1. Clean boots of dirt & seeds before hiking.
2. Carry your trash out.
3. Bury personal wastes away from streams.
4. Do washing at least 100 feet away from natural water supply.
5. Respect endangered species. DO NOT feed wild animals.

Using This Book

In the text preceding each trail description is a map to help you get to the trailhead. These maps are not exactly to scale but are drawn to emphasize important features. For each hike, I give the hike's features as well as camping information (where applicable), one-way hiking distance and time (unless otherwise noted), driving instructions, special instructions, and introductory notes about the hike.

In the trail description, I usually mention the flora and fauna along the trail, particularly the unusual and the unique, in hopes of adding to your hiking enjoyment. But I mention only a few examples, and you may wish to buy one or several small guides to plants and animals common to the islands. These are available at bookstores on the island.

Many places on Kauai are readily accessible even to the tenderfoot and to people not inclined to hike much. The hikes included in this guide are in four categories, and a glance at the Hiking Chart below will enable you to make a decision based on your interests, your skill, and the time you wish to devote to your hike. The "Family Hikes" are short, easy strolls for people

Hiking Chart

No	Trail	Family	Hardy Family	Strenuous	Difficult	Distance (miles)	Time (hours)	Elevation Gain/Loss (500 ft or more)	Good Trail	Rough Trail	No Trail	Lihue Miles	Lihue Time (hrs)	Equipment	Features
1	Kalalau Trail				X	10.8	DAY	1000	X			42	1.5	XX XX	XX XXX X X
	to Hanakapiai														
	to Hanakapiai Valley														
	to Hanakoa						See pp. 26-46								
	to Hanakoa Falls														
	to Kalalau Beach														
	to Big Pool														
2	Lumahai Beach Trail	X				0.5	0.5		X			36	1	X	XX
3	Powerline Trail				X	13	6-7	2000	X					XX XX	XXXX
	Hanalei Trailhead											32	1		
	Lihue Trailhead											12	0.5		
4	Moloaa Beach Trail	X				1.5	1				X	18	1	XX	X X
5	Nounou Mountain Trails														
	Eastside		X			1.75	1.5	1250	X			7	0.5	XX XX	X X
	Kuamoo-Nounou		X			2	1		X			8	0.5	XX XXX	X X
	Westside		X			1.5	1	1000	X			10	0.5	XX XX	X X
6	Keahua Trails														
	Keahua Arboretum	X				0.5	0.5		X			12	0.5	XX	X X
	Moalepe		X			2.5	2	700	X			12	0.5	XX XX	X X
	Kuilau Ridge		X			2.1	2	700	X			12	0.5	XX XX	X X
7	Lydgate Park	X				1	1		X			6	0.5	XX	X XXX
8	Shipwreck Beach Trail	X				2	1				X	14	1	XXX	X XX
9	Kukuiolono Park Trail	X				1	0.5				X	12	0.5	X	XX
10	Salt Pond Trail	X				0.5	0.5				X	25	1	X	X XX
11	Fort Elizabeth Trail	X				0.5	0.5		X			25	1	X	XX
12	Polihale State Park Trail	X				3	1.5				X	38	1.5	XXX	X XX
13	Waimea Canyon Trails											32	1.5		
	Iliau Nature Loop	X				0.25	0.25		X					X	X
	Kukui			X		2.5	2	2200	X					XX XX	X X
	Waimea Canyon			X		8	5-6			X				XX XX	X X
	Koaie Canyon			X		3	2	1000		X				XX XX	X X
	Waialae Canyon			X		0.3	0.5			X				XX X	X X
14	Kokee State Park Trails											38	1.75 (Park HQ to Trailhead)		
	EAST														
	Halemanu-Kokee		X			1.2	1		X			0.6		XXXXX	
	Waininiua		X			0.6	0.5		X			2.2		XXXX	
	Kumuwela		X			1	1		X			1		XXXX	X
	Puu Ka Ohelo/ Water Tank/Berry Flat		X			1.6	1.5		X			0.9		XXXXX	X
	Ditch			X		1.7	2			X		2.3		XX XX	XX
	Alakai Swamp			X		3.5	3	500		X		3		XXXXX	X
	Kawaikoi Stream		X			1.75	1.5			X		3.8		XXXXX	
	Poomau Canyon		X			0.3	0.25		X			4.5		X X	X
	Kohua Ridge			X		2.5	3	800	X			5.5		XX XX	X
	Mohihi				X	4	3	800		X		6.2		XX XX	X
	Kaluapuhi	X				1.6	1		X			1.9		XXXX	X
	Pihea			X		3.7	3	500		X		3.8		XX XX	X
	Cliff	X				0.1	0.25		X			2.1		X XX	X X
	Canyon			X		1.8	1.5	500	X			2.1		XX X	XXX X
	Black Pipe		X			0.5	0.5			X		2.5		XXXX	X
	WEST														
	Nature	X				0.1	0.25		X			Behind Museum		X	
	Milolii Ridge			X		5	3	2200	X			0.7		XX XX	X X
	Nualolo			X		3.75	3	1350	X			50 yds		XX XX	X X
	Nualolo Cliff			X		2.1	1.5		X			Off Nualolo Trail		XX XX	X X
	Awaawapuhi			X		3.25	2.5	1600	X			1.5		XX XX	X X

See pp. 26-46

with small children and people who are unaccustomed to strenuous activity. Hikes in the "Hardy Family" category require some effort, sound physical condition and children who want to hike! Hikes in the "Strenuous" and the "Difficult" classifications are more serious hikes that require sound physical condition, good footwear and outdoor skills and equipment (see Equipment section below). Most of them are full-day or overnight hikes.

The Hiking Chart provides the information necessary for a person to choose a hike. It includes one-way trail time and distance, elevation gain if more that 500 feet and equipment needed. Obviously, trail time depends on your pace and physical condition, and the time you devote to sightseeing or swimming. The time given is based on a leisurely pace, excluding time to picnic or to swim.

The trail rating in the Hiking Chart is based on whether there is a trail that is either maintained or sufficiently traveled so that it is distinguishable. However, do not be discouraged by a "rough" or "no trail" rating, for in many cases a stream or some readily identifiable physical characteristic marks the way.

Driving time and mileage are based on the posted speed limit and are measured from Lihue, the county seat (The islands of Kauai and Niihau make up Kauai County). Specific driving instructions to the trailhead appear with each hike.

Equipment

The short-term visitor and the casual hiker do not need a lot of sophisticated hiking equipment. For a day hike, the following equipment is recommended.

DAYHIKE CHECKLIST

Daypack
Hiking boots or tennis shoes
Plastic water bottle, quart size
Mirror
Swiss Army knife
Insect repellent
Shorts
Bathing suit
Sun screen and tanning lotion
Sun glasses
Whistle for each child
Camera and film
Poncho or raingear
Hat or sun visor
Towel
Waterproof matches
Hiking Kauai — The Garden Isle

Although the backpacker or overnight hiker visiting the island may have had previous experience, here are some items of equipment and some tips that should prove helpful.

BACKPACK CHECKLIST

General Equipment:

Frame and pack
Lightweight sleeping bag
    or blanket (beach camping)
Sleeping bag (over 4,000 feet)
Backpack tent with rainfly
Plastic ground cover
Sleep pad
Plastic bottle, quart size
Swiss Army knife
Flashlight
40 feet of nylon cord
First-aid kit

Cooking Gear:

Backpack stove
Fuel
Cooking pots
Sierra cup
Fork, spoon
Plastic bowl
Waterproof matches

Clothing:

Poncho or raingear
Pants, shorts or bathing suit
Hat
Bandana (doubles as washcloth)
Underwear
Socks
Hiking boots

Toilet Articles:
Soap (biodegradable)
Toothbrush/powder-paste
Part-roll of toilet paper
Chapstick
Comb
Mirror
Insect repellent
Sunscreen and tanning lotion

Miscellaneous:
Sun glasses
Camera/film
Plastic bags
Fishing gear

Although hiking boots are not essential on most hikes, I wear them because I am particularly fond of my feet, and I recommend them. Water is available from streams in many areas, but should be boiled, treated or filtered before drinking. Cattle, pigs and goats usually share the stream water with you. I suggest you begin each hike with one quart of water per person. Because of the heavy rainfall on Kauai, dry firewood is rare, so a small, light, reliable backpacking stove is a convenience and a comfort. A hot cup of tea, coffee or soup is invigorating while waiting out a passing storm, and a hot breakfast is desirable after a wet night. Lastly, most hikers find shorts adequate on most trails. However, along the Kalalau Trail some people shed all clothing for either physical or psychological reasons — I have not decided which.

Food is about 20% more expensive on Kauai than on the mainland and readily available in most communities. You may visit a local delicatessen that prepares box lunches containing local favorites such as tempura, sweet-and-sour spare ribs and sushi. When fruits are not available along the trail, be certain to visit a local market or roadside stand for mango, papaya, breadfruit, pineapple, passion fruit, and local avocado which comes in the large economy size.

Hiking and backpacking are pleasurable when the hiker has taken the time to plan his trip and to prepare his equipment.

Breadfruit

Kauai's Campgrounds

Camping on Kauai will add another dimension to your visit. Campgrounds on Kauai range from adequate to good and contain most amenities. The accompanying map locates state and county campgrounds. In addition, the Division of Forestry provides a number of wilderness campgrounds and camping shelters in Waimea Canyon that are identified on individual maps throughout the book.

The Division of State Parks regulates camping and hiking along the Na Pali Coast: Hanakapiai, Hanakoa, Kalalau — the three major valleys along the Kalalau Trail. Camping permits are $10 per person, per night and may be obtained from the Division of State Parks (address in Appendix). Camping is limited to five nights total along the Na Pali Coast in any 30-day period. Hanakapiai and Hanakoa are limited to one night each in that period.

State campgrounds are also located at Kokee and Polihale State Parks. Camping is limited to five days per 30-day period for each campground. Permits cost $5 per campsite, per night. When writing for reservations for any of the state parks, include the dates desired, the park, the number of persons and their names.

Because the State frequently changes the regulations governing hiking and camping, I recommend that you send a self-addressed stamped envelope to the Division of State parks (address in Appendix) and request current regulations and a camping application.

Secondly, the County of Kauai operates numerous campgrounds and beach parks on the island. County camping costs $3 per adult per day (Hawaii residents are free). Persons under 18 are free if accompanied by an adult. Permits are not issued to persons under 18. Camping permits are issued for up to seven days at each campsite. A total of sixty (60) camping days per year is allowed. For A Request for Camping Permit, write Department of Parks and Recreation, County of Kauai (address in Appendix). An application with detailed information will be forwarded.

Last, the Hawaii State Division of Forestry maintains a number of wilderness campgrounds in Waimea Canyon (see pp.96-7). Camping is limited to four nights within a 30-day period. All the campsites are primitive and lacking in amenities, but to some people that is their best feature. Permits are free from the Division of Forestry (address in Appendix).

Campers are well-advised to bring their own equipment because locally it is expensive. Pedal Paddle in Hanalei (address in Appendix) is well-stocked with rentals and a complete line of hiking and backpacking needs, and their staff is well-informed and helpful.

CAMPGROUNDS

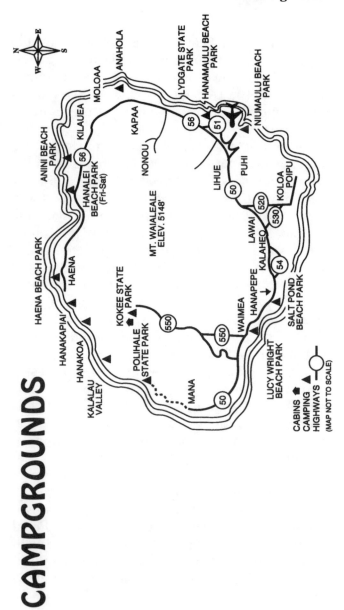

N
E
W
S

ANAHOLA
MOLOAA
KILAUEA
ANINI BEACH PARK
HANALEI BEACH PARK (Fri-Sat)
HAENA BEACH PARK
HAENA
HANAKAPIAI
HANAKOA
KALALAU VALLEY
POLIHALE STATE PARK
KOKEE STATE PARK
MANA
KAPAA
NONOU
MT. WAIALEALE ELEV. 5148'
WAIMEA
HANAPEPE
LAWAI
KALAHEO
LIHUE
PUHI
KOLOA
POIPU
LYDGATE STATE PARK
HANAMAULU BEACH PARK
NIUMAULU BEACH PARK
SALT POND BEACH PARK
LUCY WRIGHT BEACH PARK

56
51
50
520
530
54
550
550
50

CABINS
CAMPING
HIGHWAYS
(MAP NOT TO SCALE)

Camping in Hawaii has always been an enjoyable and inexpensive way to experience the Islands. Recently, however, some campers have been beaten and a few have been killed. Most of the beatings have been committed by local men, according to the victims. Most of the assaults have taken place at campgrounds that were close to cities or towns where locals congregate. There has been little or no problem in remote and wilderness areas. The best advice is to avoid camping in areas readily accessible to locals and to avoid contact with groups of people. I recommend Kokee State Park, Haena Beach Park and Salt Pond Beach Park. The latter is one of the best beach camping places in Hawaii.

Periodically, the County will close a campgound for repairs as a result of overuse or natural disasters. Therefore, check with the County prior to your visit.

Most of Kauai's drive-to campgrounds are in picturesque locations and are readily accessible. Backpacking campsites are identified on the Camping map.

Driving directions from Lihue to —

Haena Beach Park (40 Miles) Recommended
Drive north on Route #56 to Haena campground opposite the dry cave. Water, restrooms, beach showers, tables and barbecue grills are available. Sandy beach, but swimming is hazardous. Excellent snorkeling at "tunnels" about 1/2-mile east.

Hanalei Beach Park (35 miles)
Friday, Saturday & Holidays only
　　Drive north on Route #56 to Hanalei, turn right after St. Michael's Church, right at road's end past Hanalei Pavilion Beach Park until you reach the pier. Water, restrooms, beach showers, tables and barbecue grills are available. Sandy beach, but swimming is hazardous.

Anini Beach Park (25 miles) Recommended
　　Drive north on Route #56, turn right 2 miles past Kilauea after crossing a large, concrete bridge (Kalihikai), then left on Anini Road to campground. Water, restrooms, beach showers, tables and barbecue grills are available. Swimming and snorkeling are good.

Camping at Salt Pond Beach Park

Anahola Beach Park (15 miles)
NOT Recommended
    Drive north on Route #56, turn right past 13 mile marker on Anahola Road, and follow it to the campgound. Water, restrooms, beach showers.

Hanamaulu Beach Park (3 miles)
    Drive north on Route #56, Turn right   on Hanamaulu Road to beach and campground under trees. Water, restrooms, beach showers, tables and   barbecue grills are available. Swimming is fair.

Salt Pond Beach Park (25 miles) Recommended
    Drive south on Route #50 to Hanapepe, turn left on Lele Road, turn right on Lolo Kai Road to campground on the left. Water, restrooms, beach showers, tables and barbecue grills are available. Swimming and snorkeling are good.

Lucy Wright Beach Park (25 miles) Recommended
    Drive south on Route #50 to Waimea, turn left on Alawai Road after crossing the bridge over Waimea River. Campground can be seen from the highway. Water, restrooms, beach showers, tables and barbecue grills are available.

Polihale State Park (38 miles) Recommended
    Drive south on Route #50 to sign "Polihale State Park" just before highway's end. Left at the sign on a dirt/sugar-cane road for 4.7 miles to road's end. Water, restrooms, beach showers, tables and barbecue grills are available. Swimming is hazardous.

Kokee State Park (38 miles) Recommended
    Drive south on Route #50, right on Route 550
past Waimea to Kokee State Park Headquarters.
Turn left to campground at the far end of a large
meadow. Water, restrooms, showers, tables and
barbecue grills are available. Rental housekeeping cabins are also available.

Waimea Canyon Camping
    Waimea Canyon is reached via the Kukui
Trail (see pp. 96-103). Wilderness, walk-in camping is permitted in the canyon for four nights in
a 30-day period. Permits are free from the
Division of Forestry (address in Appendix).

Kokee Cabin

Kokee Housekeeping Cabins

The state rental cabins in Kokee State Park, very popular with locals and tourists, require reservations. Kokee Lodge is not really a lodge but rather 12 rustic cabins each completely furnished with refrigerator, water heater, range, cooking utensils, hot shower, linens, blankets, beds and a wood stove. All you need is food, which is not available in Kokee but 20 miles away in Waimea. There is, however, a restaurant in the lodge a short walk from the cabins. A light breakfast is served daily from 9 a.m. to 11 a.m. and lunch is offered from 11 a.m. to 3:30 p.m.

Each cabin will accommodate 3-7 persons at a modest cost from $35-$45 per day. The units vary in size from one large room, which sleeps six persons, to two-bedroom cabins that will accommodate seven. State Park rules limit a stay to five days and prohibit pets.

The cabins are very popular so make reservations early — even one year in advance is not too soon. Forward the number in your group as well as the dates you wish to reserve. Payment is refundable, less a $15 service charge, if cancellation is received at least one week prior to the reservation date. Full payment is required for confirmation. Business hours at the lodge are from 9 a.m. to 4 p.m. daily. (Address in Appendix.)

Hawaiian Made Easy

For your interest, throughout the text wherever a Hawaiian place name is used, I have provided a literal translation if possible. In many instances, Hawaiian names have multiple meanings and even the experts sometimes disagree over the literal meaning. The meanings given here are based on the best information available and on the context in which the name is used. As students of the environment, the Hawaiians had a flair for finding the most expressive words to describe their physical surroundings.

Many visitors are reluctant to try to pronounce Hawaiian words. But with a little practice and a knowledge of some simple rules, you can develop some language skill and add to your Hawaiian experience. Linguists regard Hawaiian as one of the most fluid and melodious languages of the world. There are only 12 letters in the Hawaiian alphabet: five vowels, a,e,i,o,u, and seven consonants, h,k,l,m,n,p,w. Hawaiian is spelled phonetically. Correct pronunciation is easy if you do not try to force English pronunciation onto the Hawaiian language. Vowel sounds are simple: a=ah; e=eh; i=ee; o=oh; and u=oo. Consonant sounds are the same as in English with the exception of w. Rules for w are not adhered to with any consistency by local people.

Generally, w is pronounced "w" at the beginning of a word and after a. For example, Waimea is pronounced "Wai-may-ah" and wala-wala is "Wah-lah-wah-lah." Hawaiians also usually pronounce w as "w" when it follows o or u; auwaha is "ah-oo-wah-hah," and hoowali is "hoh-oh-wah-lee." When w is next to the final letter of a word, it is variably pronounced "w" and "v"; Wahiawa is "wah-he-ah-wa," but Hawi is "ha-vee." Listen to the locals for their treatment of this sound. Since the Hawaiian language is not strongly accented, the visitor will probably be understood without employing any accent.

Some common Hawaiian Words:

'aina	land
ali'i	royalty; chief
aloha	welcome; love; farewell
aloha nui loa	much love
hale	house
haole	foreigner; Caucasian
hapa haole	part Caucasian and part ?
heiau	pre-Christian temple
hukilau	fish pull
kahili	feather standard
kahuna	priest
kai	sea
kama'aina	native-born
kane	male
kapu	keep out
kaukau	food
keiki	child

kokua	help
lua	toilet
mahalo	thanks
makai	toward the sea
malihini	newcomer
mele	song
ohana	family
'ono	delicious
'opu	belly
pali	cliff
paniolo	cowboy
pau	finished
puka	hole
pupus	snacks
wahine	female
wikiwiki	hurry

Some common Pidgin words:

brah	brother, as a term of endearment
da kine	whatchamacallit
hana hou	encore
howzit?	what's happening?
shaka!	great!
suck 'em up	drink up
talk stink	use profane words
to da max	all the way

Part II: Hiking Trails On Kauai

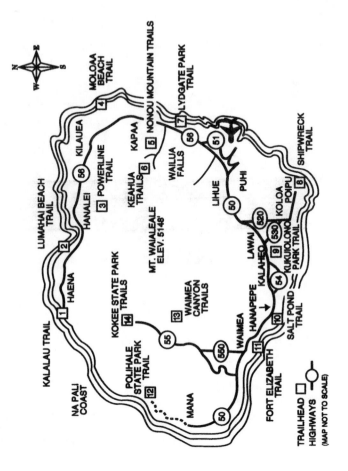

KAUAI TRAILS

KALAU TRAIL

NA PALI COAST

LUMAHAI BEACH TRAIL

HAENA

HANALEI

KILAUEA

MOLOAA BEACH TRAIL

POWERLINE TRAIL

KOKEE STATE PARK TRAILS

MT. WAIALEALE ELEV. 5148'

KEAHUA TRAILS

KAPAA

NONOU MOUNTAIN TRAILS

LYDGATE PARK TRAIL

WAILUA FALLS

SHIPWRECK TRAIL

LIHUE

PUHI

KOLOA POIPU

KUKUIOLONO PARK TRAIL

LAWAI

KALAHEO

HANAPEPE

WAIMEA CANYON TRAILS

WAIMEA

SALT POND TRAIL

FORT ELIZABETH TRAIL

POLIHALE STATE PARK TRAIL

MANA

TRAILHEAD □
HIGHWAYS ○
(MAP NOT TO SCALE)

Kalalau Trails
(Hiking Area No. 1)

Rating: See individual hikes.

Features: Wilderness area, camping, coastal views, fruits, waterfalls, swimming, historical sites.

Permission: Camping permits are required for Hanakapiai, Hanakoa and Kalalau valleys. Permits for camping must be obtained from the Division of State Parks (see Camping section in the Introduction for details and Appendix for addresses).

Hiking Distance & Time: See individual hikes.

Driving Instructions: (42 miles, 1 1/2 hour) From Lihue, drive north on Route 56 to road's end.

Introductory Notes: When people talk about hiking on Kauai, they talk about visiting the uninhabited valleys of the Na Pali (the cliffs) Coast. The Kalalau ("the straying") Trail from the trailhead at road's end at Kee Beach to the end of the beach fronting Kalalau Valley (10.8 miles) is the most exciting hike on the island.

Few who have hiked the Kalalau Trail will deny its grandeur and its captivating allure. Cliffs rise precipitously above the blue-green water and the rugged, rocky north shore of Kauai. The valleys of the Na Pali Coast are

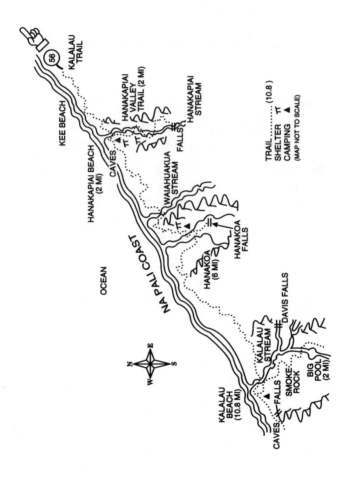

56

KALALAU
TRAIL

KEE BEACH

HANAKAPIAI
VALLEY
TRAIL (2 MI)

HANAKAPIAI
STREAM

HANAKAPIAI BEACH
(2 MI)

CAVES

WAIAHUAKUA
STREAM

HANAKAPIAI
FALLS

HANAKOA
(6 MI)

HANAKOA
FALLS

OCEAN

NA PALI COAST

DAVIS FALLS

KALALAU
STREAM

SMOKE
ROCK

BIG
POOL
(2 MI)

KALALAU
BEACH
(10.8 MI)

CAVES

FALLS

TRAIL......... (10.8)
SHELTER   ⊤⊤
CAMPING   ▲
(MAP NOT TO SCALE)

N
W—E
S

Na Pali Coast

accessible only by foot or by boat, and only during the summer when the tides expose a generous sandy beach, which is ripped away each year by winter storms.

Hiking the entire trail to Kalalau requires backpacking equipment for a comfortable, safe trip. Sound hiking boots are essential, since a good deal of your hiking is alternately on soft cinders and ash and rocks along the precipitous coast and on rocky trails in the valleys. A strong, waterproof tent is needed to stand up under the wind at Kalalau and the rain at Hanakoa.

Although fresh water is available all along the
trail, you should boil the water or purify it or use
a good filtration device; people, goats and pigs
are using the same stream. A light sleeping bag
or light blanket is adequate, particularly during
the summer months when the nighttime tem-
perature is very comfortable. Little clothing is
necessary during the day, and it is still somewhat common to find both sexes hiking without
any. A backpacking stove is recom-mended since
dry firewood is difficult to find and tree cutting is
not permitted.

Kee Beach

The trailhead for the Kalalau Trail is at the end of Route 56, where you will find several parking areas. A word of caution, however, may save some grief: vehicles left overnight in the parking places are frequently vandalized so do not leave anything in your car. Furthermore, if rental car companies learn that you are back-packing they usually won't rent to you even if you have a reservation. Hitchhiking, which is legal on Kauai, is an alternative to renting a car. Taxi service is available from the Princeville Airport.

Captain Zodiac, a commercial tour company, offers a boat shuttle service between Hanalei and Kalalau Valley. They charge about $100 round-trip per person including backpack or $55 for one-way service (see Appendix).

ON THE TRAIL:

Kee Beach to Hanakapiai Beach,
2 miles, 1 hour, 600 feet elevation gain/loss
(trail rating: hardy family).

The trek to Hanakapiai (lit., "bay sprinkling food") Beach from Kee (lit.,"avoidance") Beach is one steep mile up and one steep mile down on a wide, maintained trail. This is a much frequent-ed trail because tourist publications promise a verdant valley resplendent with native and introduced flora. No one is disappointed. Particularly abundant is the hala (Pandanus tectorius), an indigenous tree that grows in coastal areas. It is sometimes called "tourist pineapple," since the fruit resembles a pineapple and is jokingly identified as such by locals for tourists. Humor aside, the hala has been a valuable resource, the hollow trunk of the female tree being used as a pipe for drainage between taro patches. The leaves have commercial value being used for weaving many items such as baskets, mats and hats — hats being particularly popular with tourists. In the past, the fruit was eaten in times of famine and was used to make colorful necklaces. When the sections of the fruit were dried, they were used as brushes.

The first half mile up the cliff provides views at a couple of points back to Kee Beach and Haena ("wilderness") reefs. This part of the trail is usually shady because of the large trees and cool because of the trade winds and periodic rain showers. One source of shade is the large kukui (Aleurites moluccana) tree from which a beautiful and popular lei is made. To make a lei, each nut must be sanded, filed and polished to a brilliant luster that is acquired from its own oil. Until the advent of electricity, kukui-nut oil was burned for light. Nicknamed the "candlenut tree" its trunk was shaped into canoes by early Hawaiians.

The trail leads up and down from the 1/2 to the 1 1/4-mile marker. With any luck you may find some sweet guava (Psidium guajava), a small yellow, lemon-sized fruit that contains five times more vitamin C than an orange. Before eating one break it open and check for worms. They are tiny and are a little hard to see but are common in wild guava.

Hanakapiai Beach

Near the 1-mile marker, look for a small springlet that flows year round and provides a welcomed face-splashing. At the 1 1/2-mile marker, you'll have your first view of Hanakapiai Beach below, with its generous beach (during the summer months) and its crashing surf. Look for wild orchids, with their delicate purplish flowers, thriving along the banks of the trail.

As you descend to the beach, several warning signs caution visitors not to swim in the ocean because of the heavy surf and of the presence of riptides and strong currents. Several drownings occur here in spite of the posted admonition. Use the rope that extends from bank to bank to cross the stream. If the rope is not in place, be very cautious crossing. Stream rocks are uneven and very slippery. DO NOT cross if the water in the stream is rushing and high.

Camping at Hanakapiai is a pleasant experience, particularly after dayhikers have departed. Frequent rains and a lot of mosquitoes can be annoying, but the fresh water stream for bathing and the sandy beach compensate for any hardship.

Hanakapiai Valley Trail,
2 miles, 1 1/2 hours, 800 feet elevation gain/loss (trail rating: strenuous).

The Hanakapiai Valley Trail follows the stream and passes through a rain forest resplendent with native flora. The beginning of the trail

Hanakapiai Valley

on the west side of the valley contains some of the largest mango (Mangifera indica) trees anywhere. One grove surrounding the remains of a coffee mill contains a tree that is 23 feet in circumference. Obviously, it makes a shady sheltered campsite. The mango tree is not native to Hawaii, but its many varieties have done well there, and are popular with locals and tourists. However, the trees in this valley do not bear as well as those in drier areas because of a fungus that kills the blossoms in wet areas. Many people regard the mango fruit as second to none in taste and appearance.

The hike to the falls is a must not only because the falls are spectacular, but also because much serenity and enchantment are to be found in the valley. The first 1/4-mile is an easy trail that snakes along the stream. "Okolehau" ("okole" is translated "anus" or "buttocks"; and "hau" can mean "cool.") is the name of a Division of Forestry trail-crew shelter near the coffee mill which you may use when it is not occupied by a trail crew.

You will make several stream crossings depending on the time of year and the amount of rainfall. The trail is always easy to find because the valley is so narrow. However, be alert for unstable places caused by yearly heavy rains and flooding. The last 1/2-mile is the most difficult part, but perhaps the most enchanting, with inviting pools and verdant growth. The trail is cut along the walls of the canyon in a number of places. Caution is well-advised.

Although the pool at the base of the falls is inviting, caution is again advised for there is danger from falling rocks from the cliffs and the ledge above the falls. Hanakapiai Falls cascades and falls about 300 feet in the back of a natural amphitheater. You don't need to be told to swim and enjoy the pools and the surrounding area. You will find safe pools away from falling rocks.

Hanakapiai to Hanakoa,
4 miles, 2 1/2 hours, 800 feet elevation gain/loss (trail rating: strenuous).

Serious hiking on the trail to Kalalau Valley begins at this point as the trail climbs out of Hanakapiai Valley on a series of switchbacks for one mile. This is the most difficult section of the

Mangoes - soooo good!

entire 11-mile trek. Hiking here in the morning means that the sun will be at your back and, with the trade wind, it should be relatively cool. The trail does not drop to sea level again until Kalalau Beach, some eight miles along the cliffs.

There are two small valleys before Hanakoa. The first is Hoolulu (lit., "to lie in sheltered waters"), which is first viewed from a cut in the mountain at the 3 1/4-mile marker. From here you descend to cross the valley and climb the opposite side. Hoolulu is thickly foliated with native and introduced plants that are typical of most valleys on the island. Ti, guava, morning glory, mountain orchids, and different kinds of ferns can be identified along with the larger kukui, koa and hala trees. Be careful at points where the trail narrows along a precipitous slope.

Waiahuakua Valley, at the 4 1/4-mile marker, is broader than Hoolulu. In June-August, you are likely to find delicious ohia ai (Eugenia malaccensis), or mountain apples, growing along the trail. Abundant in Waiahuakua, these trees have smooth, dark green leaves and some attain a height of 50 feet. The fruit is a small red or pinkish apple with a thin, waxen skin, while the meat is flesh-white, crisp and juicy, with a large brown seed in the center — a very tasty repast for those lucky enough to find some. Additionally, the valley abounds in coffee, ti, guava, kukui, and mango.

At the 5 3/4-mile marker, you will get your first view of Hanakoa (lit., "bay of koa trees or of warriors") Valley which is a broad-terraced valley that was once cultivated by Hawaiians. Many of the terraced areas provide relatively sheltered camping sites. In addition, "Mango Shelter" has a roof and table, and "Hanakoa Shack," a short distance away, is a Division of Forestry trail-crew shelter that is open to hikers when not in use by crews. Camping in Hanakoa is quite an experience since it receives frequent rains, and as soon as you dry out, it rains again. So, if you plan to camp in Hanakoa, you should be prepared for a lot of rain, wetness and humidity. To compensate, you will have solitude and a private swimming pool if you camp away from where the trail crosses the stream. The afternoon can be warm and sunny, just perfect for a swim in one of the many pools in the stream and a sunbath on the large, warm rocks along the bank. These are a favorite of nude sun worshippers.

To Hanakoa Falls,
0.4 mile, 1/4 hour.

The trail begins between the stream crossing and the 6 1/2-mile marker and passes a wilderness campsite and terraced areas once used by the Hawaiians for growing taro from which the staple food poi is produced. Expect the route to the falls to be overgrown and laden with rocks and boulders as a result of frequent floods in the valley. The falls cascade down the pali in a breathtaking setting.

Kalalau Valley

Hanakoa to Kalalau Beach,
4.8 miles, 3 hours, 800 feet elevation gain/loss
(trail rating: strenuous).

Your physical condition and your hiking skill
will be tested on the remainder of the trail. Most
of the trail traverses switchbacks that pass in
and out and up and down through several
gulches. At a number of places, the trail narrows
along a very precipitous cliff where a misstep can

result in a serious mishap. Another hazard is the hot afternoon sun unless you begin hiking early. However, the views of the northwest coastline are absolutely breathtaking and staggeringly beautiful. It is difficult to think of another view in the world that compares.

At the 6 1/2-mile marker, you enter land that until 1975 was part of the Makaweli (lit., "fearful features") cattle ranch owned by the Robinson Family who also own the island of Niihau off the coast of Kauai. The area becomes increasingly dry as you continue west, and only the smaller more arid types of vegetation survive, like sisal and lantana. Lantana (Lantana camara) is a popular flower that blossoms almost continuously. Its flowers vary in color from yellow to orange to pink to red; infrequently, they are white with a yellow center. If you hike in the early morning or late afternoon you're likely to frighten feral goats foraging near the trail and near some of the small streams along the trail.

Although there are only a few trail-mileage markers over the rest of the route, there is no chance of getting lost. The trail is over open land and visible ahead. There are at least five reliable sources of water between Hanakoa and Kalalau. The admonition to treat, filter or to boil the water applies.

Pohakuao (lit., "day stone") is the last small valley before Kalalau. As you ascend the west side of Pohakuao along a pali with sparse foliage and reddish earth, you reach Red Hill, as it is known to locals, from which you get your first

view of Kalalau, a welcome sight after three difficult miles from Hanakoa. There is no mistak-
ing Kalalau, for it is a large, broad valley some
two miles wide and three miles long. From the
ridge, a precipitous snake-like trail drops
abruptly to Kalalau Stream where rushing
water and cool pools await the weary hiker.

Camping is allowed on the beach, in the trees
fronting the beach and in the caves at the far
end of the beach. Try to find a spot that will shelter you from the strong winds and the hot day-
time sun. Some campers find shelter in the low
scrub along the beach during the day and then
sleep on the beach during the cool and usually
wind-free nights. Lantana and common guava
are particularly abundant along the trail in the
beach area. You should easily find some ripe
guava to add to your meals. Don't drink the
stream water until you treat, filter or boil the
water. The falls at the end of the beach by the
caves is the most convenient source of water. Be
certain to treat, filter or boil the water. The
water from the falls also serves the feral goats
that you will undoubtedly see in the morning
and at dusk when they visit to refresh them-
selves. Most of the campers take a daily shower
under the falls.

Kalalau abounds in a variety of life. Beach
naupaka (Scaevola frutescens), with small, fragrant, white flowers, can be found near the
beach, mixed with the low sisal and lantana.
Hala, ti, ferns, bamboo, bananas, mango, kukui,
monkeypod and many other species of flora can

be identified. Rock terraces where Hawaiians planted taro as late as the 1920s are also common.

Kalalau Beach to Big Pool,
2 miles, 1 1/2 hour, 1000 feet elevation gain/loss (trail rating, hardy family).

The trail into the valley begins on the west side of Kalalau Stream at the marked trailhead. Before heading into the valley, hike to the top of

Zodiac pickup at Kalalau Beach

the knoll above the beach, also on the west side of the stream. The remains of a heiau — a pre-Christian place of worship — lie between the knoll and the beach and are clearly identifiable from this vantage point. Little is known about this nameless heiau. Remember that such places are still revered by many people and should be respected.

From the trailhead, the trail parallels the stream for a short distance and then ascends an eroded rise. From here the trail alternately passes open and forested areas. In the wooded areas look for oranges, mango, common guava and rose apple. Each can be found in the valley and can supplement a backpacker's diet. At the one-mile point, Smoke Rock is a convenient place to pause in an open area from which the entire valley can be viewed. This is the place where the valley marijuana growers and residents used to meet to smoke and to talk story. The rest of the trail to Big Pool is under the shade of giant mango and rose apple trees. The latter bears a small,edible, pale-yellow fruit. Before reaching Big Pool, a side stream crossing must be made. Heading into the valley, the next stream crossing is Kalalau Stream. Big Pool, a short distance from this crossing, is easily identified. Two room-sized pools are separated by a natural water slide which is a joy to slip down into the cool water below. It's a delightful place to enjoy the sights and smells of Kalalau, Kauai's most precious treasure.

The Folk Hero of Kalalau

Locals and visitors enjoy speculating about the exploits and the hideouts of Kalalau's most famous citizen, Koolau. Commonly called "Koolau the Leper," this native Hawaiian was born in Kekaha in 1862. Three years after showing signs of leprosy, at the age of 27, Koolau and the other lepers of Kauai were ordered to the leper colony on Molokai, and were promised that their wives and children could accompany them. When the ship sailed without his wife and child, Koolau, realizing he had been tricked, dove overboard and swam ashore. Together with his wife and child he made the perilous descent into Kalalau Valley to join other lepers who sought to escape deportation. A year later, local authorities decided to round up the lepers, all of whom agreed to go to Molokai except Koolau. A sheriff's posse exchanged fire with Koolau, who shot and killed a deputy. Martial law was declared, and a detachment of the national guard was sent from Honolulu with orders to get their man dead or alive. A small cannon was mounted near the site where Koolau was thought to be hiding. In the ensuing "battle" Koolau shot two guardsmen and one accidentally shot and killed himself fleeing the leper. The remaining guardsmen fled from the valley to the beach. In the morning they blasted Koolau's hideout with their cannon. Believing him dead, the guardsmen left the valley. But Koolau had moved his family the night before the cannonading, and they lived in the valley for about five more years, always fearful that the guard was still looking for him. They hid during the day and hunted for food at night. Tragically, their son developed signs of leprosy and soon died; a year later, the dread disease claimed Koolau. Piilani, his wife, buried her husband in the valley that had become their home along with his gun which had enabled them to be together to the end.

To some, Koolau is a folk hero who received unfair treatment by the government. Indeed, locals claim that Koolau frequently left his valley hideout to visit friends and relatives on Kauai. Whatever the facts, it makes for an interesting story and campfire conversation.

No one that I have met has ever been disappointed by their Kalalau experience.

Food – Coconuts

Lumahai Beach Trail

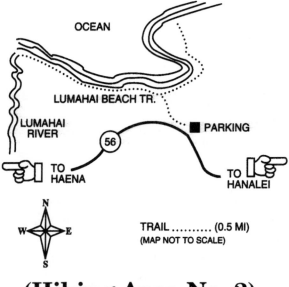

OCEAN

LUMAHAI BEACH TR.

LUMAHAI RIVER

56

■ PARKING

TO HAENA

TO HANALEI

N
W E
S

TRAIL .... (0.5 MI)
(MAP NOT TO SCALE)

(Hiking Area No. 2)

Rating: Family.

Features: Beachcombing, shelling, picnic, views.

Permission: None.

Hiking Distance & Time: 0.5 mile, 30 minutes.

Driving Instructions: (36 miles, 1 hour) From Lihue, drive north on Route 56 past Hanalei. Lumahai Beach is on the west side of Hanalei Bay just before the 6-mile marker where the road makes a sweeping "U" turn with a wide shoulder on the ocean side. Park off the road and remove all valuables from your car. Unfortunately, even locked cars have not stopped thieves.

Introductory Notes: Lumahai (lit., "a certain twist of the fingers in making string figures") Beach is a short, pleasant walk and picnic spot. Lumahai is regarded as the most beautiful beach on Kauai. It is certainly one of the most photographed, appearing in tourist papers and on calendars throughout the world. It has also appeared in many movies, most notable "South Pacific" (1957) where Hollywood star Mitzi Gaynor was filmed singing "I'm Going to Wash That Man Right Out of My Hair." The trail is a pleasant beach walk and a place to work on your tan.

In 2001, The Trust for Public Land purchased the 40 acre beach from longtime owner, the Wilcox Family. The property was then conveyed by the Trust to the State of Hawaii to be managed as a public resource. In accepting the property, Governor Ben Cayetano ackowledged the The Trust's many contributions to the people of Hawaii. He said, "Today, we add Lumahai Beach to a String of Pearls system of state parks throughout the islands that we have set aside to protect for generations to come."

On the Trail: The trail drops about 50 feet to the beach as it passes through a pandanus grove. Under the shade of the hala, or screwpine (Pandanus odoratissimus), is an idyllic spot to picnic. As previously noted, the hala is frequently called "tourist pineapple" since the fruit resembles a pineapple. The fruit is sometimes cut into sections, which are then strung to make a fruit lei. The leaves, called lauhala, are dried and woven into mats and hats which are popular for beach and casual wear.

Ironwood trees also front the beach and afford a measure of shade and protection from the hot sun. In spite of its appearance, the ironwood is not a pine — conifer. The "needles" are branchlets that never develop into leaves, but they do make a comfortable cushion.

Stroll west to the mouth of the Lumahai River and to the east to a the massive black, lava rock formation where you'll find several tide pools. Examine their contents, but be aware of the waves that frequently leap over the rocks. Locals can sometime be found searching the sand for puka (hole) shells to be used for making necklaces. The shells are the broken tops of mollusks and are found in a variety of sizes. The highly prized Niihau shell has also been found here. These are tiny, sometimes slightly colored shells that are commercially very expensive. A one-strand necklace sized properly can range in price from $300 to $1,000.

Lumahai Beach is a delightful spot to picnic and to find a measure of solitude.

Swimming should be approached with CAUTION due to the strong offshore currents. If you choose to swim, be certain to stay within the offshore rocks. Several drownings are reported here annually.

Powerline Trail
(Hiking Area No. 3)

Rating: Strenuous.

Features: Fruit, views, native and introduced flora and fauna.

Permission: None.

Hiking Distance & Time: 13 miles, 6-7 hours, 2,000 feet elevation gain/loss.

Driving Instructions:
—To Hanalei Trailhead (32 miles, 1 hour) Drive north on Route 56 past Princeville Airport, turn left onto Pooku Road and drive 1.7 miles to end of pavement. Park off the road.
—To Lihue Trailhead (12 miles, 1/2 hour) From Lihue, drive north on Route 56, turn left on Route 580 to University of Hawaii Agriculture Experiment Station and turn left and drive to Keahua Stream and Arboretum. Drive through the stream for 0.2 mile to dirt road and hunter's check station on the right. Park off the road.

Introductory Notes: The powerline trail is exactly what the name implies. The road was built to facilitate the construction of power trans-mission lines between Lihue and Hanalei. Some evidence suggests, however, that the route was originally an early Hawaiian trail link between the two communities.

Both the Hanalei and Lihue trailheads are readily accessible (see map and Driving Instructions above). Typically, this is a solitary hike over a deeply rutted dirt road where you will need to negotiate mud and water-filled mud holes. This full day hike requires sound footwear, two quarts of water per person, food and essential equipment noted in the Introduction. For personal safety, wear bright clothing while hiking, particularly during hunting season. Hunting is generally open only on weekends and state holidays, but all hunters may not respect the rules.

You will be richly rewarded if you choose to hike just a few miles or an hour or so from either trailhead. Families with small children will find the first few miles from the Hanalei Trailhead easy going.

On the Trail from Hanalei: From the off-road parking area at pavement's end, a water tank is visible about 100 yards up the trail. The telephone poles and lines are the only unsightly things to intrude on the lushly foliated surroundings. Initially, the trail makes a gentle ascent, levels out and then dips and rises throughout. Yellow, lemon-sized common guava and strawberry guava — red, golf-ball sized fruit — are plentiful throughout the hike. DO NOT, however, pursue fruit off the trail for the underfooting is uncertain and can be dangerous.

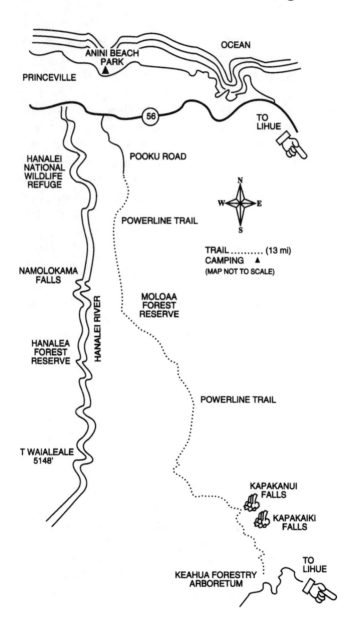

OCEAN

ANINI BEACH
PARK

PRINCEVILLE

56

TO
LIHUE

POOKU ROAD

HANALEI
NATIONAL
WILDLIFE
REFUGE

POWERLINE TRAIL

N
W   E
S

TRAIL .... (13 mi)
CAMPING   ▲
(MAP NOT TO SCALE)

NAMOLOKAMA
FALLS

MOLOAA
FOREST
RESERVE

HANALEI RIVER

HANALEA
FOREST
RESERVE

POWERLINE TRAIL

T WAIALEALE
5148'

KAPAKANUI
FALLS

KAPAKAIKI
FALLS

TO
LIHUE

KEAHUA FORESTRY
ARBORETUM

Strawberry Guava

A break in the trees near the 1/2-mile point affords a view to the west (right) of Hanalei, the Hanalei River and the Hanalei National Wildlife Refuge. The latter is home to several rare, endemic birds such as the Koloa, a Hawaiian duck, (Anas wyvilliana), the Common Moorhen (Gallinula chloropus sandvicensis) and the Black-necked Stilt (Himantopus mexicanus knudseni) each of which is on the federal endangered species list. Trailside, hau (Hibiscus tiliaceus) with its dense tangle of limbs and yellow-flowered hibiscus and the native ohia lehua (Metrosideros collina) with its tufted red stamens are readily identifiable.

At the one-mile point and from several vistas thereafter numerous waterfalls come into view, the highest of which is Namolokama (Lit., "the interweaving bound fast") Falls plunging several hundred feet from the west pali from Namolokama Mountain. Indeed, depending on rainfall, several other falls will be visible. The falling water rushes to the valley floor and is carried via the Hanalei River to the sea. Verdant Hanalei Valley at your feet is a sight beyond description. The trail bisects the Hanalea Forest Reserve to the west (right) and the Moloaa Forest Reserve to the east (left).

As you proceed into the interior, the trail follows the eastern edge of the hunting area so that the likelihood of coming across feral pigs or goats on the trail increases. Both are timid and more than likely will rush off into the brush when you approach. Goats pose little or no threat to humans and pigs usually will only attack if they feel threatened. I have found that noise and hand clapping frightens them. You are more likely to come across hunter's dogs who are working well ahead of their master or are heading home. I know of no hiker who has been attacked by these dogs. Recently, mountain bike riders have discovered the powerline trail so that bikers, invariably covered with red dirt and mud, may be encountered on the hike.

Throughout the hike, numerous trails/roads branch off your trail. Most lead to power poles and lines while others are used as turnouts for heavy equipment. You'll find pipes, poles and line scattered indiscriminately trailside.

At about midpoint, you'll come across a dilapidated shack that was once used by workers, hunters and hikers.

Beyond the shack the trail ascends to the highest point at Kualapa (2128 feet) from which it seems possible to reach out and touch Mt Waialeale (5148 feet) to the southeast. However, cloud cover may prohibit a view. Waialeale (lit., "overflowing water") is the wettest place on earth receiving and average of 465 inches of rain annually. Kawaikini (Lit., "multitudinous water"), just south of Waialeale is the highest point on the island at 5,243 feet. You have probably donned your poncho while enjoying countless waterfalls that seemingly drop hundreds of feet to the base of the valley and the headwaters of the Hanalei River. It's an awesome sight.

Shortly, the trail jogs southeast on a ridge with Keahua (lit., "the mound") Stream below on your left and Uhauiole (Lit., "rat-hitting") Stream on your right. I have found the remaining 2-3 miles to trail's end to be very wet with countless deep, muddy pools. Be alert for a break in the vegetation to the northeast (left side) of the trail for a view of Kapakanui (Lit., "large raindrop") Falls (left) and Kapakaiki (Lit., "small raindrop") Falls (right).

The last 100 yards is a steep descent to the Lihue trailhead. At the trailhead, turn left and walk 0.2 mile to Keahua Arboretum for a refreshing swim in the stream (see Hike No. 6).

Moloaa Beach Trail

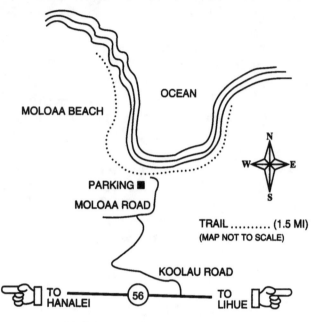

(Hiking Area No. 4)

Rating: Family.

Features: Swimming, shelling, beachcombing, fishing, fruits, views.

Permission: None.

Hiking Distance & Time: 1.5 miles, 1 hour.

Driving Instructions: (18 miles, 3/4 hour) From Lihue, drive north on Route 56, just past 16-mile marker, turn right on Koolau Road and drive 1.2 miles, and then turn right on Moloaa Road to end. Park along beach right-of-way.

Introductory Notes: The Moloaa (lit., "matted roots" - said to be of the paper mulberry growing here) Beach hike is included here because it is one of the more secluded beaches on the island — a place where you can explore, fish, hunt for shells and swim. You can search the beach for shells and, with some luck, you might find a glass-ball or plastic float used by Japanese fishermen on their nets. Some break loose and make the long journey to Kauai.

Check the mango trees along Moloaa Road for ripe fruit. Unfortunately, most of the fruit is out of reach unless you have a fruit picker — a bamboo pole with a cloth basket attached to a loop at one end. Many locals carry a pole that can be extended like a fishing rod and folded when not in use. If you drive Moloaa Road at night, perhaps you shouldn't carry fresh pork. Even some present-day Hawaiians believe that the demigod Kamapuaa, who is part pig, part man, still lives in the valley and will assume a variety of shapes and attack if he smells fresh pork. He can be outwitted, however, if the meat is wrapped in ti leaves.

On the Trail: The trail along the northwest side of the bay, a fisherman's trail, leads to some of the best spots from which to cast. Usually you need to walk out on the coral. Before you do, however, sit on the bank a while and watch the ocean to study the surf conditions. The only com-

pany you are likely to have is an occasional fisherman or the cattle or horses that graze on the
slopes.

On the upper slopes you can identify the
paper mulberry (Broussonetia papyrifera) from
which the name of the area is derived. It is a
small tree with lobed leaves covered with woolly
hairs on the undersides of the leaves. The bark
of the plant was an important source of tapa, the
cloth of ancient Hawaii. Tapa was made by
removing the outer bark of the tree and soaking
and beating the inner bark. A carved wooden
mallet was used to pound the fibers until they
became thin and flexible. Sheets were joined by
the same pounding process, usually performed
by men, while the women would decorate the
cloth using a block printing method or leaves
dipped in dye and pressed on the cloth.

The trail on the east side of the bay also
snakes along the coast and provides a number of
places to fish, picnic or simply enjoy the solitude.
Check the shoreline for glass or plastic floats,
shells and driftwood.

Nounou Mountain Trails (Sleeping Giant)

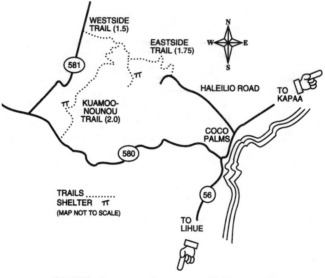

(Hiking Area No. 5)

Rating: Hardy Family.

Features: Views of Kauai, fruits.

Permission: None.

Hiking Distance & Time: Consult individual hikes.

Driving Instructions:
(see instructions preceding each hike below).

Puni - The "Friendly Giant"

Introductory Notes: It is told that the giant
Puni lived among the legendary small folk, the
Menehune, but was so clumsy that he continual-
ly knocked down their homes and their stone
walls. Nevertheless, he was so friendly that the
Menehune could not help liking him. One day
the little people were faced with an invasion, and
they went to the giant in the hope that he would
destroy their enemies. However, they found him
asleep on a ridge near Kapaa (lit., "the solid or
the closing"). In an effort to awaken him, they
threw large rocks on his stomach, which
rebounded toward the ocean, destroying some of
the invading canoes and causing the others to

flee. In the morning they tried to awaken Puni again, only to discover that some of the rocks they had thrown at him had landed in his mouth. Tragically, he had swallowed them and died in his sleep.

There are three routes to the summit of Nounou (lit., "throwing") Mountain which are good, well-maintained trails that will take you to the giant's chin and to his forehead. Nounou is truly one of the best hikes on Kauai. Be sure to carry at least one quart of water, since it is a hot hike in spite of frequent trade winds.

If you have a second vehicle, I recommend hiking the East-side Trail to the summit and then return via the West-side Trail to the junction with the Kuamoo-Nounou Trail and follow it to highway 580 — 5.3 miles — (see map).

Nounou Mtn. - EAST
1.75 miles, 1 1/2 hours, 1,250 ft. elevation gain/loss (trail rating: hardy family).

Driving Instructions: (7 miles, 1/2 hour) From Lihue, drive north on Route 56 past Coco Palms Hotel, turn left on Haleilio Road and drive 1.2 miles to a parking area off the road on the right by the sign "Nounou Trail."

On the Trail: The trailhead is to the right as you drive into the parking area. The trail is a series of well-defined switchbacks along the northeast side of the mountain. Pause frequently and enjoy the vistas overlooking the east side of Kauai. Below you lie the Wailua Houselots,

while the Wailua River is to your front right.
There are 1/4-mile trail markers along the entire
route.

The large trees that flourish in the area not
only offer a relatively shady trail but also provide some shelter from showers. You will find
strawberry guava, passion fruit, ti, tree ferns, a
variety of eucalyptus, and other flora that
deserve special note.

The hau (Hibiscus tiliaceus) tree is of partic-
ular interest not only because of its pretty
bright-yellow blossom but also because of its
long, sinuous branches that interlock to form an
impenetrable barrier. Locals jokingly note that
the tree is appropriately named (hau, pronounced how) because where they are plentiful,
no one knows "hau" to pass through!

On a spacious overlook at about the one-mile
point, you can rest in the shade of the ironwood
(Casuarina equisetifolia) tree, which resembles a
pine because of its long, slender, drooping, dull-
green "needles", but it is not a conifer. It is an
introduced tree that has a long life and is very
useful as a windbreak or shade tree.

Just beyond the 1 1/2-mile marker, the
west-side trail merges with ours for the ascent
to the summit. Alii (lit., "chief") Shelter and
table at the 1 3/4-mile marker is a pleasant
place to picnic and to enjoy the panorama of the
island and the solitude. There are a number of
benches near the shelter that provide comfortable places to meditate. You should see a white-
tailed tropic bird (Phaethon lepturus) as it

soars along the mountainside with its conspicuous 16-inch tail streamers.

From the shelter, walk south about 20 yards past monkeypod trees and survey the trail that leads to the giant's "chin," "nose" and "forehead." Be CAUTIOUS, if you choose to continue, because you must walk across a narrow ridge above a nearly vertical 500-foot cliff, scramble up about 50 feet on your hands and knees to the "chin" and walk on a narrow ridge about 150 yards to the "forehead." From all points of the giant's anatomy, the views are outstanding. Look below the giant's chin for a hole through which the wind rushes.

Kuamoo-Nounou Trail,
2 miles, 1 hour
(trail rating: hardy family).

Driving Instructions: (8 miles, 1/2 hour) From Lihue, drive north on Route 56, turn left on Route 580 (Kuamoo Road) to 5750 Kuamoo Road. The trailhead on the right side of the road.

This trail is a pleasant hike even if you don't hike to the summit of Nounou Mountain. Most of the trail passes under a canopy of native and introduced trees and a picnic shelter near the midpoint affords a panoramic view of the valley and the mountains beyond. The trail is wide with 1/4-mile markers to trail's end.

On the Trail: Initially, the trail passes between a residence on the left and pasture on the right before dropping to a wooden bridge over

Opaekaa Stream. Look for ripe common (yellow)
and strawberry guava along the stream and
throughout the hike. Both trees are prolific and,
when in season, the aroma from rotting fruit
underfoot is intoxicating. From the bridge, the
trail swings left and begins a gradual ascent
under a canopy of hau trees, a variety of hibiscus
bearing bright yellow blossoms.

Valley Vista trail shelter is 0.75-mile from
the trailhead on a perch overlooking Wailua
Homesteads to the west, Kawaikini (Kauai's
highest point at 5,243 feet) beyond and the
Makaleha Mountains to the northwest.
Generally, numerous waterfalls are visible.

On the trail

The trail continues an easy rise to the 1-mile marker before beginning a gradual descent to the junction with the West-side trail at the 1.8-mile point. More guava to enjoy, a patch of bamboo, eucalyptus trees and a grove of giant Norfolk Island pines (Araucaria excelsa) are here to enjoy. The latter are tall, perfectly symmetrical trees whose trunks have been used for masts on ships and as Christmas trees by island residents.

The Kuamoo-Nounou Trail meets the West-side Trail after 2-miles from where it's one mile east (right) to the junction with the East-side Trail and then 1/2-mile to the summit. The West-side Trail goes west (left) down the mountain 0.5-mile to Kamalu Road.

West-side Trail,
1.5 miles, 1 hour, 1,000 feet elevation gain/loss (trail rating: hardy family).

Driving Instructions: (10 miles, 1/2 hour) From Lihue, drive north on Route 56, turn left on Route 580 and then go right on Route 581 (Kamalu Road) for 1.2 miles to sign "Nounou Trail" on right side opposite 1055 Kamalu Road.

The West-side Trail is a bit shorter and not as steep, and offers more shade than the East-side Trail.

On the Trail: This trail passes by Queen's Acres and across a cattle range before entering the forest reserve. You will hike through a variety of introduced trees much like those found on the east side.

Look for the wild, or Philippine, orchid
(Spathoglottis plicata). The wild variety is usually lavender, with what appear to be five star-
like petals, but are actually two petals and three
sepals.

The trail reaches a junction with the
Kuamoo-Nounou Trail after 0.5 mile. Kuamoo-
Nounou Trail goes south (right) for 1.8 miles to
Route 580 and your trail (West-side Trail) climbs
another mile to join with the East-side Trail from
which it's a short trek to Alii Shelter and then to
the summit (see East-side Trail description for
details).

On top of "Old Puni"

Keahua Trails

(Hiking Area No. 6)

Rating: See individual hikes.

Features: Swimming hole, native and introduced plants, fruits, picnic shelters.

Permission: None.

Hiking Distance & Time: See individual hikes.

Driving Instructions: (see instructions preceding each hike below).

Introductory Notes: The three hiking trails in the Keahua area offer some pleasurable experiences. They offer some marvelous views of the eastside coastline and of the Makaleha

Mountains. Since the Moalepe Trail intersects
the Kuilau Ridge Trail, you have an opportunity
to follow the latter trail to Keahua Arboretum
where you can hike the Arboretum Trail and
enjoy a delightful swimming hole.

I recommend hiking the Moalepe Trail to the
Kuilau Ridge Trial and following it to the
Arboretum — 4.6 miles (see map).

Keahua Arboretum,
0.5 miles, 1/2 hour, (hike rating: family).

Driving Instructions: —To Keahua Arboretum
and Kuilau trails (12 miles, 1/2 hour) From
Lihue, drive north on Route 56, turn left on

Keahua Stream

Route 580 and drive to the University of Hawaii Agriculture Experiment Station and go left (1.8 miles) to Keahua Stream. Kuilau Ridge Trailhead is on the right at a small turnout just before the stream and Keahua Arboretum Trailhead is on the left just past the stream opposite a parking area.

Introductory Notes: Keahua (lit., "the mound") Arboretum is a project of the Hawaii State Department of Land and Natural Resources, Division of Forestry. Here is a good chance to view a variety of native and introduced plants and to swim in a cool, fresh-water pool. The arboretum receives an annual average rainfall of 95 inches. The State Forest Reserve area extends west to the top of Mt. Waialeale ("overflowing water"), the wettest place on earth, with an average annual rainfall of 465 inches. It once received a record 628 inches!

On the trail: The trail begins opposite the parking lot under a canopy of painted gum (Eucalyptus deglupta) trees with a colorful bark. This tree species is native to the Philippines and New Guinea. Behind the painted gum trees are rose gum (Eucalyptus grandis), a tree from Australia and less colorful than the painted gum. Several other trees are easy to identify here. Two of them are kukui (Aleurites moluccana) and milo (Thespesia populnea). Kukui trees, also called candlenut trees, had several uses. The most noteworthy use was the burning of its oily nuts for a light source. Kukui is Hawaii's State

Tree and identifiable by its pale green leaf and its walnut-sized nuts. Today, as in old Hawaii, the wood of the milo tree is prized for its use in making beautiful umekes, or calabashes.

The trail passes several picnic shelters and parallels the stream and several good swimming holes. The Makaleha Mountains to the west are the source watershed for the domestic water supply. Rain falling on the mountains percolates into the soil and is collected in tunnels for distribution into the county water system. Good forest cover increases infiltration of water into the soil. This not only helps to increase the ground water supply but it also helps prevent soil erosion and floods caused by surface run-off.

One of the most conspicuous trees along the trail is the hau (Hibiscus tiliaceus) whose dense tangle of limbs prohibits entry. This yellow-flowered hibiscus was an early Hawaiian introduced plant. Here, you will also find the most common native tree species in Hawaii, the ohia lehua (Metrosideros collina). Early Hawaiian uses for the wood of the ohia included house timbers, poi boards, idols and kapa beaters. In the early 1900's, railroad ties hewn from ohia logs were exported for use on the mainland. A favorite of Madame Pele (the goddess of volcanoes) the ohia is easily identifiable by its tufted red stamens that remind the visitor of the bottlebrush tree.

Streams in this forest reserve provide a home for native and introduced fish. The native Hawaiian oopu lives here as well as smallmouth

Hala - "Tourist Pineapple"

bass. Fresh-water Tahitian prawns, esteemed as a delicious food, can also be found here.

As you approach the swimming hole, notice the native hala tree commonly called "tourist pineapple." Its stilt-like trunk and its fruit that resembles a pineapple make this tree easy to identify. The trail descends the hill where you can return to your car or, better yet, go to the stream for a swim. There is usually a rope suspended from a mango tree on the bank about 100 yards from the shelter. It's a fun place.

Arboretum rope swing

Moalepe Trail,
2.5 miles, 2 hours, 700 ft. elevation gain/loss
(hike rating: hardy family).

Driving Instructions: —To Moalepe Trail (12
miles,1/2 hour) From Lihue, drive north on
Route 56, turn left on Route 580, go right for 1.6
miles on Route 581 to Olohena Road and turn
left for 1.7 miles to where the road makes a
sharp right turn onto Waipouli Road. Trailhead
is posted at the head of a dirt road.

On the trail: Do not attempt to drive beyond the
Olohena-Waipouli Road intersection because the
road is deeply rutted and, when wet, very slippery. The first part of the trail is on a right-of-
way dirt road over pasture land. The usually
cloud-enshrouded Makaleha (lit., "eyes looking

about as in wonder and admiration") Mountains rise majestically to the northwest. In fact, the State of Hawaii, Division of Forestry, which is in charge of the area, has plans to extend the trail to the top of the Makalehas. Be sure to pause to enjoy the panorama of the coastline, from Moloaa on the north to Lihue on the south. There are some guavas along the fence and even more in the pasture, which is private land. The trail is a popular equestrian route with riders who rent horses from the ranches in the area: evidence of this fact can be found on the trail!

The first mile is a gentle ascent in open country. Then the trail enters the forest reserve. Hereafter, the trail is bordered with a variety of plants and trees, including the wild, or Philippine, orchid, different types of ferns, eucalyptus trees and the popular ohia lehua, with its pretty red blossoms. In the forest reserve the road-trail narrows and begins to twist and turn along the ridge, with many small and heavily foliated gulches to the left and Moalepe (lit., "chick with comb") Valley to the right. You can expect rain and therefore a muddy trail to the end of the hike. The trail reaches a junction with the Kuilau Ridge trail on a flat, open area at the 2- mile point. The Ridge Trail to the south (left) descends to a trail shelter and eventually ends at Keahua Arboretum, 2.1 miles from the junction. From the junction, the Moalepe Trail is a footpath that snakes northwestward a short distance to a lookout point from which an enchanting panorama awaits the hiker.

Kuilau Ridge Trail,
2.1 miles, 2 hours, 700 ft. elevation gain/loss
(trail rating: hardy family).

Driving Instructions: (see Keahua Arboretum
above for instructions).

On the Trail: One of the most scenic hiking trails
on the island, the Kuilau ("to string together leaves
or grass") Ridge Trail climbs the ridge from Keahua
Arboretum. From the trailhead to trail's end, an
abundance of native and introduced plants greets
the hiker. The ascent of the ridge is on a well-maintained foot and horse trail lined with hala, ti plants,
from which hula skirts are fashioned, and the very
pretty lavender wild, or Philippine orchid. But the
best prize is a couple of mountain apple trees on the
left side of the trail a short distance up from the
trailhead. Perhaps you'll find some apples, which
are red or pink when ripe.

At the 1 1/4-mile point the trail reaches a
large flat area and a trail shelter and a picnic
site. It is a delightful place to pause to enjoy
views of the many heavily foliated gulches and
the Makaleha Mountains beyond. The trail
beyond the shelter passes through one of the
most beautiful places on the whole island. The
Kuilau Ridge Trail twists and turns on a razor-
back ridge past a number of small waterfalls. It is
a treasure to savor. Before reaching the shelter,
the trail crosses a footbridge at the bottom of a
verdant gulch and then ascends the ridge to a
large flat area. From here, the trail continues 0.2
mile to its junction with the Moalepe Trail.

Lydgate State Park Trail

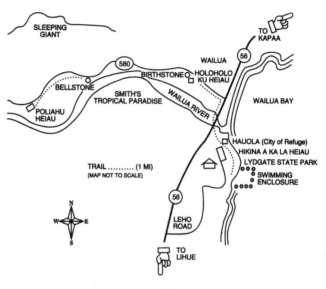

(Hiking Area No. 7)

Rating: Family.

Features: Swimming, snorkeling, heiaus, a place of refuge, picnicking, fruits.

Permission: None.

Hiking Distance & Time: 1 mile, 1 hour.
Driving Instructions: (6 miles, 1/2 hour) From Lihue, drive north on Route 56 to the 5-mile marker, turn right on Leho Dr., and go right on Nalu Road to the pavilion.

Introductory Notes: Throughout the hike, it's easy to understand why early people settled here. Fertile soil, fresh water, plentiful fish and a long sandy beach to land their canoes supported a large population. Today, Lydgate Park and Wailua River State Park offer a passage into the lives of these ancient people. Your trail passes through a city of refuge, three heiaus, birthstones and a bell stone, all important sites for an understanding of traditional Hawaiian life. Both parks remain a favorite of locals and visitors since they offer an understanding of old Hawaii, a hike through history, safe swimming, snorkeling and picnicking.

On the Trail: Your trail begins in Lydgate Park, a large, football-field-sized expanse of greenery between the ocean and the Holiday Inn Sunspree Resort. Children will enjoy the play area containing hi-tech apparatus — rope ladders, rope swings, wood bridges, and an assortment of buildings. A striking, lava rock/wood pavilion offers picnic tables and drinking water. Weddings and luaus are frequently conducted in the pavilion.

If you begin at daybreak, you may be fortunate enough to find glass ball floats (more recently plastic), which are highly prized by locals, who will even search for them at night with lanterns. Most of these floats are from the nets of Japanese fishermen, so they have traveled thousands of miles. Some have been found more than 30 inches in circumference.

Temple of Refuge

The park's swimming enclosure is the only safe place to swim. There are strong currents outside the enclosure and an unusually heavy surf. Frequently, the rescue squad is called to help ocean swimmers in distress who fail to heed the warning signs on the beach. The most famous of all rescues took place when Frank Sinatra was pulled from the surf by some local boys.

Between the swimming enclosure and the Wailua (lit., "two waters") River are the remains of Hauola (Lit., "dew of life") a Temple of Refuge, a place of importance in old Hawaii and Hikina A Ka La Heiau (Lit., "rising of the sun"). Each island had a place of refuge where those who had been vanquished in battle, violators of taboos and noncombatants could find safety from capture or

punishment. These havens were respected by all.
After a period of time and prayer, the individual
could return home — a very humane concept and
practice. Such places were important in ancient
Hawaii for the kings and ali'i (chiefs) were all
powerful and governed according to a kapu
(taboo) system, rigidly enforced to control politi-
cal, social and religious activity. Anyone violating
their rules met with swift and certain justice.

Hikina A Ka La Heiau is adjacent to the
refuge. It was given this name because the first
rays of the sun in the Wailua area touch here
each day. Large rocks outline the site. Little
remains of either except for a metal marker identifying the refuge and an assortment of boulders
scattered under the shade of giant coconut trees.

From here it is a short hike to the bridge
spanning the Wailua River. Pause on the bridge
and look for the flat bottom, motorized boats that
ferry passengers upriver to the world famous
Fern Grotto, a popular site for weddings and
tourists who take the 2 mile trip to visit the fern-
draped cave. Commercial kayak outings and
water skiing are common on the river too.
Looking northwest from the bridge, Puni, the
sleeping giant, reclines on his back seemingly
presiding over the eastside.

Continue walking over the bridge to Route
580, that passes between the river and the Coco
Palms Resort. From the junction with Route 56,
follow Route 580 for 0.2 mile to Holo-Holo-Ku
(lit., "to run-and-stand") Heiau (a place of worship) on the left side of the road. Heiaus played

an important part in pre-Christian Hawaiian culture. There are hundreds of known heiaus on the Islands that served specifically to ensure rain, good crops, or success in war, while others were used for human sacrifice. Here you'll find a large sacrificial stone forming the southwest corner of the heiau. As you stroll through the heiau bear in mind that it is a religious place and should be respected as such.

At one time royal birthstones, a priest's house, and reproductions of idols were in the heiau. The originals are to be found in the Bishop Museum in Honolulu. Royal birthstones were important in ancient Hawaii. Pregnant women in the royal family would give birth in huts next to the birthstones to ensure the royal status of an unborn infant.

Follow the sign to a small public cemetery behind the heiau which contains a number of interesting lava headstones, some of which date back to the last century.

A large mango tree across the road should be checked for fresh fruit, although the mangoes may be inaccessible unless you have a picker. The large, pear-shaped fruit with orange pulp is quite sweet and juicy in season — usually March to October. Look under the tree for those that have fallen and are not too badly bruised, or find a stick to shake some loose from the tree. The wood from these large, beautiful trees has been used for crafts wood, furniture and gun stocks.

The road's shoulder is too narrow to walk safely to the ruins of Poliahu Heiau located one mile farther up Route 580 on the left side of the road overlooking the Wailua River, so it is best to drive to the site.

Many generations ago, stones from the river below were carried by hand to this bluff to build Poliahu (Lit., "garment for the bosom") Heiau. Over the years, it was remodeled and changed by the chiefs and priests to meet their needs. Structures within the walls were destroyed in 1819 when the traditional religion was abolished.

Walk east (toward the ocean) paralleling the highway to a rough dirt road and then a path that leads to two large boulders and a path between them that leads to a bellstone which was struck by the priests to announce the birth of a royal member. When properly struck, a bellstone could resonate for miles.

From the heiau, it's a short walk across the highway for a view of Opaekaa (rolling shrimp) Falls. Fresh water shrimp are still found in the river.

Snorkeling

Shipwreck Beach Trail

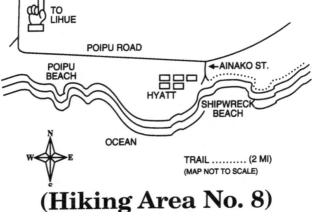

(Hiking Area No. 8)

Rating: Family.

Features: Surfing, body boarding, tidepools, views.

Permission: None.

Hiking Distance & Time: 2 miles, 1 hour.

Driving Instuctions: (14 miles, 3/4 hour) From Lihue, drive south on Route 50, turn left on Route 520, go right on Route 530 and make a quick left on Poipu Beach Road. Drive to Hyatt Kauai and turn right past the hotel on Ainako St. to a public parking lot on the right fronting the beach.

Introductory Notes: Poipu (lit., "completely overcast of crashing — as waves") Beach is perhaps the finest swimming and snorkeling place on Kauai. And Keoniloa Bay or Shipwreck Beach as it is known by locals a mile east from Poipu and fronting the Hyatt Kauai Resort is one of the best surfing and body boarding beaches, where the big waves give you an exhilarating ride. When you see the beach, you'll probably pass on hiking. Aquamarine water, warm and seemingly pristine white sand and awesome looking girls and guys, make Shipwreck Beach an ideal place to spread a towel and enjoy the ambiance.

On the Trail: No trail as such exists. Walk out to the water and follow the coastline northeast (left) to a promontory at beach's end. The under-footing to the top is brittle and broken so be cautious. From the summit you'll enjoy a panoramic view of the most recent volcanic eruption on Kauai, about 40,000 years ago! Young in geologic time anyway, the area is dotted with numerous cinder cones and lava tubes, which some say extend to the ocean. Indeed, as you walk you can sometime hear and feel the rushing water underfoot. DO NOT walk close to the edge since the underfooting is uncertain and the drop is vertical to the sea.

From here, you can amble along for a few miles or less. All the plants here struggle for survival in an area where the rainfall is light and the soil extremely porous. Ilima (Sida fallax) is a small, woody shrub that grows wild. With its small, blunt, bright green leaves and its pale orange, orange or brown flowers, it makes a popular lei. In earlier times only members of the royalty were allowed to wear an ilima lei.

The strong wind has bent and twisted the ironwood (Casuarina equisetifolia) trees in a variety of interesting shapes.The tree resembles a pine because of its long, slender, drooping, dull-green branchlets, but it is not a conifer.

You'll find numerous pipes to cradle fishing poles buried in the soft rock close to the edge of the bluff. Fishermen are frequently present in the morning or evening hours and are usually eager to talk story. Visitors are frequently surprised to discover that many local residents have traveled extensively.

Your hike ends when you choose to end it. Return to the beach and enjoy the sights, tide-pools and a splash in the surf. This is not a safe swimming beach.

Plumeria blossoms

Kukuiolono Park Trail

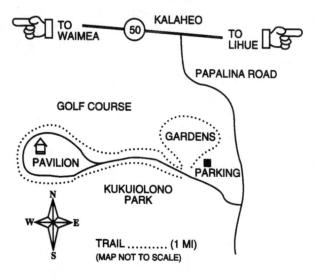

(Hiking Area No. 9)

Rating: Family.

Features: Japanese Garden, picnic, views.

Permission: None.

Hiking Distance & Time: 1 mile, 1/2 hour.

Driving Instructions: (12 miles, 1/2 hour) From Lihue, drive south on Route 50 to Kalaheo, turn left on Papalina Road and drive 1 mile to the park gate. Turn right into the park and park by the gardens.

Introductory Notes: Walter McBryde, son of one of the earliest European settlers on Kauai, built his home and an elegant park on this hill above the town of Kalaheo (lit., "the proud day") and overlooking Lawai (lit., "seaward") and the beautiful south coast. During World War ll, the "Big House" of the McBrydes was used to billet U.S. military officers who were on leave. The house burned down many years ago.Today, the McBryde estate is a private park and a popular spot to golf, picnic, and stroll through a Japanese garden. Kukuiolono (lit., "the light of the god Lono") is so named because the hill was used by ancient Hawaiians to signal fishermen at sea and to serve as a beacon.

On the Trail: Park by the garden and take the short, interesting, pleasant loop around the gardens. The legendary stones of the Hawaiians are particularly notable. The name of each stone indicates its use or significance. For example, there are Lono's Spoon Stone, Awa (fish) Stone, Kauai Iki (little Kauai) Stone (shaped like Kauai), Stone Bowl and Stone Salt Pan. Most are three to four feet in circumference. There are also a number of smaller "game stones" which were used in Hawaiian games similar to bowling and the shotput.

The flora in the garden is a mixture of native and introduced plants and trees: crotons, mangoes, kukuis, bananas, papayas, tree ferns, sego pines, and other types of pines, to name a few. The most striking sights are the intricate and delicate-

Stone bowling ball

ly beautiful bonsai plants and the flowing "dry stream" of white stone that passes through the garden.

From the garden, walk up the road to the pavilion. You will enjoy the plumeria (Plumeria acutifolia) trees along the road. Every color and shade of plumeria seems to be represented. Perhaps the most popular of all lei flowers, the thick, velvety flowers have a delightful fragrance. The white, yellow, pink and cerise plumerias are overwhelming when in full bloom. The milky juice, however, is poisonous and will stain clothing.

The road passes through the golf course, so be on the lookout for flying white balls. You will find water, picnic tables, shelter, and restrooms in the pavilion at the summit.

Salt Pond Trail

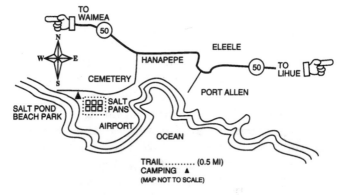

(Hiking Area No. 10)

Rating: Family.

Features: Historic salt pans, swimming, camping, shelling, tide pools.

Permission: None to hike, but county permit to camp (see Appendix).

Hiking Distance & Time: 0.5 mile, 1/2 hour.

Driving Instructions: (25 miles, 1 hour) From Lihue, drive south on Route 50 to Hanapepe, turn left on Lele Road and turn right past a cemetery onto Lolo Kai Road to Salt Pond Beach Park on the left.

Introductory Notes: Salt Pond Beach Park is one of the best camping spots in Hawaii. New facilities, a picturesque beach and a convenient location recommend it.

On the Trail: The salt ponds are east between the beach park and the airport. No trail exists, so make your way to the flat land and the conspicuous salt pans. Salt pans dug in the red soil have been passed through many generations. Hopefully, someone will be tending his pans and will explain and demonstrate the method for you. It's a simple process, but the art is practiced with pride. Sea water is placed in the pan and allowed to evaporate. Then the contents are moved to other pans to allow for thorough drying. Salt for cooking, for medicinal purposes and for the table has been produced here for generations.

Swimming here is usually safe unless otherwise posted. Typically, a county lifeguard is on duty. The beach fronting the salt pond contains a number of tide pools worthy of examination. Shellers are likely to find prized and very expensive Niihau shells at the west end of the beach. You may find residents scooping the gravel at water's edge with a kitchen colander, dumping the contents above the water line and searching the contents for the tiny and ofttimes slightly colored Niihau shells.

Salt Pond is an idyllic place to share with loved ones or a good book.

Fort Elizabeth Trail

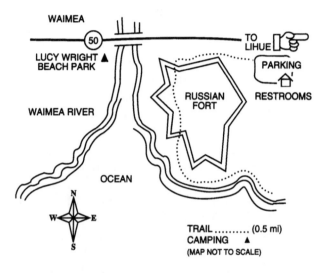

(Hiking Area No. 11)

Rating: Family.

Features: Historic site, driftwood, swimming, views.

Permission: None.

Hiking Distance & Time: 0.5 mile, 1/2 hour.

Driving Instructions: (25 miles, 1 hour) From Lihue, drive south on Route 50 to sign "Fort Elizabeth" on the left just before the Waimea River.

Introductory Notes: In 1817 the Russians secured a foothold on the islands with the construction of a fort that overlooked the Waimea (lit., "reddish water") River and the sea. To build the fort's walls, a dry-construction method was used whereby rocks are fitted according to shape, without mortar. The State of Hawaii has constructed an interpretive exhibit at the trailhead on which a trail guide to the fort can be found. Across the river on the west side is the town of Waimea and the site of Captain Cook's first landing in Hawaii.

On the Trail: A path leads from the display along the north side of the fort to the river and then into the fort. The thick walls of the fort enable the visitor to walk on top of them for the best view of the fort. A strong imagination is necessary to mentally reconstruct the fort, for the walls and the interior are in disrepair after many years of neglect. A trail snakes through the remains of the fort to the south side, and to the mouth of the river and the beach. One can easily see the commanding position of the fort.

Both inside and outside the fort are a variety and abundance of dried flowers and an assortment of dried "weeds" that make a pretty floral arrangement. Hike from the mouth of the river along the gray-black sand beach where you may find interesting driftwood.

Offshore to the southwest lies the tiny island of Niihau, part of Kauai County, which is privately owned by the Robinson family, whose ancestor bought the island for $10,000 in 1864 from the Hawaiian monarchy. Some point to Niihau as the last place where pure Hawaiians live as their ancestors did. Others, applying today's standards, assert that the people live primitively and under some hardship. The controversy is heightened by the fact the outside world is mostly excluded; visits are by invitation only.

Be certain to return to the bridge for impressive views up the river into Waimea Canyon.

On the walls - Russian fort

Polihale State Park Trail

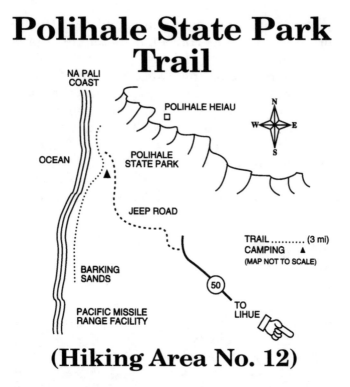

(Hiking Area No. 12)

Rating: Hardy family.

Features: Camping, swimming, heiau.

Permission: Camping permits from State Parks (see Appendix).

Hiking Distance & Time: 3 miles, 1 1/2 hours.

Driving Instructions: (38 miles, 1 1/2 hours) From Lihue, drive south on Route 50 to a sign "Polihale State Park" just before the end of the highway. Turn left at the sign and follow the dirt/sugar-cane road for 4.7 miles to the park.

Beach camping - the best!

Introductory Notes: Polihale (lit., "house bosom") State Park is a relatively secluded place to camp. As at all state parks, camping costs $5.00 per camp site and is limited to five days per month. In recent years, some campers have been violated by local men here so that you should be cautious. DO NOT camp alone and secure your valuables.

This was once the site of a famous heiau — a pre-Christian place of worship. The remains, in the form of distinctive rock piles, can be seen along the slopes of the cliffs above the park. Here you can enjoy the sunset and the view of the island of Niihau and Lehua to its right. The latter is in fact a big rock. In legend Lehua is considered to have been the first landing place of Pele, the fire goddess. The name comes from the story that Pele's sister, Hiiaka, placed a lei of lehua blossoms on it.

On the Trail: From the camping area, it is a hot
3-mile hike south to Barking Sands beach.
Unless you are a sun worshipper, sun protection
is well-advised since there is no relief from the
hot sun. Wear shorts or hike in a bathing suit
for you will want to splash in the surf.
Swimming should be approached with CAU-
TION for the sea can be treacherous, with riptides most of the year.

The beach on the way to the sand dunes is
somewhat isolated and, therefore, uncrowded. In
fact, you probably will not see another person
until you reach Barking Sands. Military personnel and their guests visit the dunes from the U.S.
Navy missile facility just south of Barking Sands.

The Barking Sand dunes are easy to identify,
for some are as high as 60 feet and about 1/2
mile in area. The name "barking sands" comes
from the idea that the sand can be made to give
off a dog-like "bark" or "woof" sound. Some visitors have not "heard" a sound and therefore
doubt the whole notion, while others insist that
they have "heard" a sound, whatever it is.
Whatever the fact, try your luck. One of the following methods may be successful for you. 1)
Find a dry dune and slide down on foot. While
sliding, listen for a deep, sonorous "woofing"
sound. 2) Fill a bottle about two-thirds full with
sand, shake it, and listen for a sound. 3) Stomp
up and down on the side of any dune. After try-
ing all these methods, you are either pleased
and fascinated by the "sounds" that you heard or
you feel like a damn fool!

Playtime at Waipoo Falls

Waimea Canyon Trails

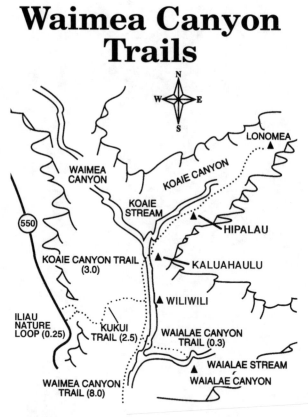

(Hiking Area No. 13)

Rating: See individual hikes.

Features: Views of Waimea Canyon, wilderness hiking and camping, swimming, native and introduced flora and fauna.

Permission: Overnight hiking and camping is permitted in the canyon for four nights in a 30-day period. Permits are required and are free from the Division of Forestry (address in Appendix). Dayhikers do not need a permit, but should leave a note in their car indicating their hiking plan.

Hiking Distance & Time: See individual hikes.

Driving Instructions: (32 miles, 1 1/2 hours) From Lihue, drive south on Route 50, turn right on Route 550 to the Kukui Trailhead on right side just past the 8-mile marker.

Introductory Notes: Waimea (lit., "reddish water") Canyon has been called the "Grand Canyon of the Pacific." Everyone I know is enthralled by the beauty and grandeur of the Canyon. It is about one mile wide, 3600 feet deep, and 10 miles long. While it does not match the magnificence of the Grand Canyon in Arizona, it has its own unique magic, with its verdant valleys, its lush tropical forest and its rare birds and flora.

Iliau Nature Loop,
0.25 mile, 1/4 hour
(hike rating: family).

The nature loop is a good place to see some 20 endemic plants including the rare iliau (Wilkesia gymnoxiphium). There is no missing the iliau since hundreds flourish in a small area. A relative to the equally rare Maui silversword, the iliau is endemic to Kauai. It grows 4-12 feet high,

Rare Iliau blossom

it is unbranched, and the stems end in clumps of
long, narrow leaves 6-16 inches long. Once in its
life, the plant flowers in a flourish of hundreds of
tiny yellow blossoms.

The trail provides a number of vistas for view-
ing the canyon and Waialae (lit., "mudhen water")
Falls on the opposite, west wall of the canyon.

Kukui Trail,
2.5 miles, 2 hours, 2,200 feet elevation loss/gain
(hike rating: strenuous).

The Kukui (candlenut lamp) Trail is really
the only trail into Waimea Canyon (I DO NOT
recommend the Waimea Canyon Trail - see
below). A Division of Forestry sign marks the

Kukui Trailhead

trailhead both at the state highway and at the departure point off the Iliau Trail. Overnight hiking and camping in the canyon is by permit issued by the Division of Forestry (address in Appendix).

The trail drops over 2000 feet into the canyon. The first half is open so that sun protection and a hat are advisable. If you hike during the heat of the day, I am certain you would rather be standing under Waialae Falls which can be seen tumbling from the pali across the canyon. About 0.3 mile down the trail, look for a wooded gulch on the left where several hibiscus (Hibiscus waimeae) trees are growing. This variety is an endemic tree that bears large white flowers that are so fragrant you can smell them from a distance.

You'll probably find numerous half-gallon plastic jugs along the trail. They are left by pig and goat hunters as they descend so they will have fresh water on their return. For safety reasons you should stay out of the brush and wear bright clothing so that you won't be mistaken for a goat or pig by hunters.

The first part of the hike offers some spectacular views of Waimea Canyon and the second part passes through heavy growth until it emerges at Wiliwili (a native tree bearing red seeds that make pretty necklaces) Campground along the boulder-laden banks of Waimea River. It is a delightful spot to camp in shade with ample water nearby. Many hikers make a base camp at Wiliwili and then hike on the canyon trails and in the side canyons. If you are in good hiking condition, it is possible to make the hike in and out in one day. There is ample water in the canyon, but it should be treated, filtered or boiled before drinking.

Waimea Canyon Trail,
8 miles, 5-6 hours
(trail rating: strenuous).
Trailhead is in Waimea Canyon.

I do not recommend the Waimea Canyon Trail. It passes through the hot, dry lower portion of Waimea Canyon. Neither the terrain nor the vegetation is interesting.

You reach the trail by hiking down the Kukui Trail to the river, or by hiking eight miles upriver from Waimea town.

The Waimea Canyon Trail travels south from the end of the Kukui Trail and parallels the Waimea River through the canyon to Makua Powerhouse. The trail then makes several crossings of the Waimea River enroute. The trail is easy to follow, but it's a very hot, dusty trek.

There is usually ample water in the canyon, but it should be treated, filtered or boiled before drinking.

Koaie Canyon Trail,
3 miles, 2 hours, 1000 feet elevation loss/gain (hike rating: strenuous).
Trailhead is in Waimea Canyon.

Koaie Canyon is a favorite of hikers and backpackers, for it's a pleasant, foliated trail that leads to a secluded wilderness shelter. The canyon's name comes from the koaie (Acacia koaie) tree, which is endemic to the islands and is much like the koa tree. The wood, however, is harder than koa wood, and was once used to make spears and fancy paddles.

If the water is high in the river, DO NOT CROSS. Flash flooding is an ever-present danger. It is necessary to cross the river to the east side to reach the Koaie Canyon Trail. You cross the river about a half mile up river just below Poo Kaeha, a prominent hill about 500 feet above the river. Kaluahaulu Campground and your trail parallels the river on the east side into Koaie Canyon.

The canyon is a fertile area that was once extensively farmed, as is evidenced by the many terraced areas you'll observe and the rock walls and the remains of house sites. You can usually find ample pools in the stream to swim in or at least to cool off in. During the summer months, the water is usually low, but sufficient for some relief from the hot canyon. The Division of Forestry maintains two wildland campsites here; one site at Hipalau and another at Lonomea Camp, an open shelter with a table alongside the stream near a generous pool for swimming at trail's end. The Lonomea (Sapindus cahuensis) is a native tree with ovate leaves which reaches heights of up to 30 feet. They grow only on Kauai and Oahu.

There is usually ample water in the canyon, but it should be treated, filtered or boiled before drinking.

Don't forget to pack out your trash.

Waialae Canyon Trail,
0.3 mile, 1/2 hour (trail rating: strenuous).
Trailhead in Waimea Canyon.

Walk south about one-half mile along the Waimea River from the campground at the terminus of the Kukui Trail to a marker that identifies the point where you can ford the river and enter lower Waialae Canyon. CAUTION; DO NOT CROSS the river when the water level is high.

This short, undeveloped trail takes you east into Waialae Canyon. The trail follows the north side of Waialae Stream for a short distance to "Poachers Camp," where a shelter, table and pit toilets are located. You're likely to meet hunters in Waialae Canyon and you're likely to see evidence of their success by the bones and the carcasses of animals left along the trail.

There is usually ample water in the canyon, but it should be treated, filtered or boiled before drinking.

Koaie Canyon Trail - Stream Crossing

Kokee State Park
(Hiking Area No. 14)

Rating: See individual hikes.

Features: Views of Waimea Canyon, Na Pali Coast and Kalalau Valley; swimming, camping, waterfalls, iliau plant, rain forest, wilderness hiking, fruit and native and introduced flora and fauna.

Permission: Camping permits from State Parks and cabin reservations from Kokee Ventures (see Appendix).

Hiking Distance & Time: See individual hikes. Driving Instructions: (38 miles, 1 3/4 hours) From Lihue, drive south on Route 50, turn right on Route 550 (Waimea Canyon Drive) to Kokee State Park Headquarters.

Introductory Notes: Kokee (lit., "to bend or to wind") State Park hiking trails rank in my top five list of favorite hiking places in the 50th State. Because the area typically receives storms and heavy rain throughout the year, trails and roads may become flooded, washed out and closed. Before hiking, check with Kokee Museum personnel for trail conditions. Many trails pass through heavily vegetated and wooded places so hikers are cautioned to STAY on established trails. Carry appropriate equipment (see pp. 10-2) and DO NOT drink stream water unless it is boiled or properly treated.

Kokee Housekeeping Cabins

The state cabins at Kokee are operated by a private concessionaire. The cabins are not luxurious, but they are comfortable. Nestled beneath giant trees, the twelve rustic cabins are completely furnished with refrigerator, water heater, range, cooking utensils, shower, linens, blankets, beds and fireplace. All you need is food, which is not available in the park, but 20 miles away in Waimea. There is, however, a restaurant a short walk from the cabins, open for a light breakfast from 9 a.m. to 11 p.m.and for lunch from 11 a.m. to 3:30 p.m.

Each cabin will accommodate 3-7 persons at a very modest cost from $35-45 per day. The units vary in size from one large room, which sleeps six persons, to two-bedroom cabins that will accommodate seven. State park rules limit a stay to five days and prohibit pets.

The cabins are very popular with locals, so make reservations early — even one year in advance is not too soon. Forward the number in your group as well as the dates you wish to reserve. Payment is refundable, less a $15 service charge, if cancellation is received at least one week prior to the reservation date.Full payment is required for confirmation. Business hours are from 9 a.m. to 4 p.m. daily. Write Kokee Ventures for complete information and reservations (see Appendix).

Kokee Camping

At the north end of a shady, picturesque meadow, tent and trailer camping are available in the shade of tall eucalyptus trees. Camping cost $5 per campsite and is limited to five days in a 30-day period. (address for state parks in Appendix). Water, tables, barbecues, restrooms and cold-water showers are available.

The Division of Forestry maintains two wilderness camping areas, one at Sugi Grove and the other at Kawaikoi (see p.108). Permit is from the Division of Forestry (address in Appendix).

In recent years a controversy has existed over the future of the Kokee-Waimea area. Conservationists have sought Federal legislation to establish a national park so that the wilderness can be preserved in relatively pristine condition. Opponents of this proposal seek to retain the present status, because a national park would probably prohibit hunting, land leases for vacation cabins and taking plants.

Whatever the future, whether your interest is hiking, hunting or sightseeing, no trip to Kauai is complete without a visit to Kokee and Waimea Canyon. Kokee is the home of the rare mokihana berry (see the Pihea Trail), and the even rarer and beautiful iliau plant (see the Iliau Nature Loop Trail) and the delicious Methley plum, which is ready for picking throughout the park in late May or early June. The picking season is short because local people flock to the park and carry off buckets full of this delectable fruit. In recent years, pickings have been poor because so many trees have been damaged by hurricanes and harvesters while others have been overwhelmed by other vegetation.

On the Trail: For safety, hikers should sign in and out in the registry at the Kokee State Park Headquarters. Your interests, physical condition, and length of stay at Kokee will determine which hike you take. On the whole, trails in the general vicinity of park headquarters are relatively short and easy, while trails into Waimea Canyon, to the valley overlooks or into the Alakai Swamp are full-day or overnight trips. Access to most of the trails is from jeep roads that radiate off the main highway — Route 550. You should not travel these roads in a passenger car even when dry, because many are steep and deeply rutted. The ranger at park headquarters and the museum personnel are the best sources of information about road and trail conditions.

The trails in the Kokee State Park/Waimea Canyon area have been worked, brushed, posted, and taped so that most are in good condition. Trail improvement programs have involved hundreds of student workers, unpaid volunteers, the Hawaii Sierra Club, and the State Division of Forestry.

All trail milage cited is one-way. The mileage from Park Headquarters to the trailhead via the most direct road is noted preceding each trail description.

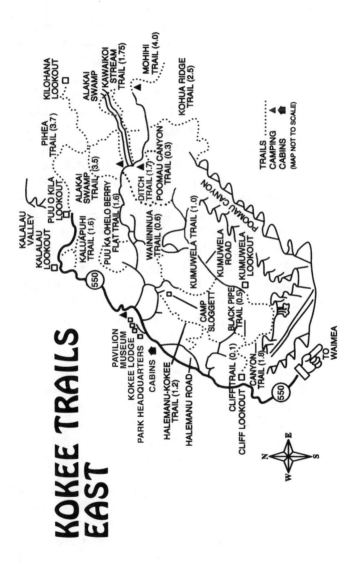

KOKEE TRAILS EAST

KILOHANA LOOKOUT

KAWAIKOI STREAM TRAIL (1.75)

MOHIHI TRAIL (4.0)

ALAKAI SWAMP

KOHUA RIDGE TRAIL (2.5)

PIHEA TRAIL (3.7)

ALAKAI SWAMP TRAIL (3.5)

PUU O KILA LOOKOUT

DITCH TRAIL (1.7)

POOMAU CANYON TRAIL (0.3)

KALALAU VALLEY

KALALAU LOOKOUT

KALUAPUHI TRAIL (1.6)

PUU KA OHELO BERRY FLAT TRAIL (1.6)

WAININUA TRAIL (0.6)

KUMUWELA TRAIL (1.0)

POOMAU CANYON

KUMUWELA ROAD

KUMUWELA LOOKOUT

550

PAVILION

MUSEUM

KOKEE LODGE

PARK HEADQUARTERS

CABINS

CAMP SLOGGETT

BLACK PIPE TRAIL (0.5)

HALEMANU-KOKEE TRAIL (1.2)

HALEMANU ROAD

CLIFF TRAIL (0.1)

CLIFF LOOKOUT

CANYON TRAIL (1.8)

TO WAIMEA

550

TRAILS ....

CAMPING

CABINS

(MAP NOT TO SCALE)

N E S W

Halemanu-Kokee Trail,
1.2 miles, 1 hour (hike rating: hardy family).
Park HQ to trailhead 0.6 mile.

This trail starts just before entering Camp Slogget near the old ranger station and ends on Halemanu Road. It's a hike for those who are interested in a short, pleasant, easy walk with the prospect of seeing some native birds and plants. The trail, linking Mohihi and Halemanu Roads, is an enjoyable hike in itself and also a route to hiking areas on Kokee's west side.

Tall trees dominate the area, such as lehua and the majestic koa. There are three red birds that you can expect to see along the trail. The cardinal has a pronounced crest, which is the most prominent feature distinguishing it from the apapane (Himatione sanguinea), a deep-crimson bird with black wings and tail and a slightly curved black bill, and the iiwi (Vestiaria coccinea), a vermilion bird with black wings and tail and orange legs. The latter also has a rather pronounced curved salmon bill. Unless you get a good look at these birds, it is difficult to identify them, but they can be enjoyed without being identified. One other bird that is common throughout the forest is the elepaio (Chasiempis sanwichensis), an endemic bird that is gray-backed with a rather long, blackish tail and white rump. It is a somewhat noisy bird, giving forth with what is best described as a sort of "wolf-whistle."

Waininiua Trail,
0.6 mile, 1/2 hour (hike rating: hardy family).
Park HQ to trailhead 2.2 miles.

Mostly a short, flat, scenic forest walk, the Waininiua Trail with the Kumuwela Trail completes a loop off Kumuwela Road. There are a variety of native and introduced plants, the most notable being aromatic ginger with its lovely, light-yellow blossoms. Many local girls like to put a fresh ginger blossom in their hair, not only for its beauty but also for its fragrance.

Kumuwela Trail,
1.0 mile, 1 hour, (hike rating: hardy family).
Park HQ to trailhead 1.0 mile.

At the end of the short spur road off Mohihi Road (see map) turn left into the forest for the beginning of the Kumuwela Trail. The trailhead is marked and the trail is well-maintained. The trail dips abruptly into a luxuriant, fern-lined gulch where Kahili ginger (Hedychium coronarium) flourishes. The size, fragrance and light-yellow blossoms overwhelm most visitors. You should find many places on and off the trail where feral pigs have been digging to get at roots.

Along this verdant trail there are also specimens of lantana, lilikoi (passion fruit) as well as handsome kukui and koa trees. The last 0.3 mile requires a 300-foot elevation gain to Kumuwela Road, where you can connect with the Canyon Trail.

Puu Ka Ohelo/Water Tank/Berry Flat Trails,

1.6 miles, 1 1/2 hours (hike rating: hardy family).
Park HQ to trailhead 0.9 mile.

These three trails combine for an easy, pleasant hike off Mohihi (a variety of sweet potato) Road. The Puu Ka Ohelo (Ohelo hill), Tank and Berry Flat trails are clear, broad and easy to follow. You will cross a couple of small streams along this verdant trail. The banana passion fruit (Passiflora mollissima) is found here draping from the trees. It is a wild vine that produces a pretty, light-pink blossom and a small, yellow, banana-shaped fruit. The vine is a pest because it smothers native trees.

The trails pass through scenic forest containing mostly introduced trees that should be easy to identify. There are stands of Australian eucalyptus, Japanese Sugi pines and the native koa (Acacia koa), which grows to a height of more that 50 feet. The koa has a light gray bark that is smooth on young trees and considerably furrowed on mature trees. The leaves are smooth, stiff and crescent-shaped. Often called Hawaiian mahogany, the wood is red with a wavy grain that makes it popular for use in furniture, woodwork and ukuleles. In older times it had nobler purposes, having been used for war canoes, surfboards and calabashes.

Particularly noteworthy is a stand of California redwoods (Sequoia simpervirens) that will excite the senses. These wondrous giants

tower over the other trees adding a certain
majesty to the grove and their droppings provide
a luxuriant carpet on which to walk. They are
found as you begin the Berry Flat Trail.

The prize to be sought here is the popular
Methley plum that flourishes in the Kokee area.
However, plum picking has been poor in recent
years because of storm damage to the trees. Look
for plum trees whose fruit ripens at the end of
May or the first part of June.

There is also a variety of birds along both
trails. (All bookstores on the island have small,
pocket-sized, inexpensive bird books featuring
the most frequently seen birds.) The cardinal
(Richmondena cardinalis) is a commonly seen
bird on the island which was introduced from the
mainland. The male, with his all-red body and
pointed crest, has been seen along the trail as
well as throughout the park.

Ditch Trail,
1.7 miles,
2 hours (hike rating: strenuous).
Park HQ to trailhead 2.3 miles.

The Ditch Trail was built during the construction of the Kokee irrigation ditch. The trail
follows a circuitous route along a cliff and in and
out of numerous gulches and small stream
canyons and connects the Mohihi Road with the
Kumuwela Road on the outskirts of the Alakai
Swamp.

The trail offers spectacular sights of the interior of Waimea Canyon, one of the broader and

deeper of the canyons found here. Numerous waterfalls and cascades, particularly during periods of heavy rainfall, drop from Kohua Ridge across the canyon .

Awini ("sharp, bold, forward") Falls is at the southwest tip of the ridge, with Mohihi Falls to the right-rear of the canyon and Moeloa ("to oversleep") Falls to the left-rear of the canyon.

The trail is rich with flora, from the common guava to lehua and a variety of ferns. The variety of tree fern (Cibotium menziesii) seen here is the "monkey's tail" fern, with its wiry black hairs on the frond stems. It has the biggest trunk of all Hawaiian tree ferns, a trunk often used for carving akuas (idols) or tikis.

Alakai Swamp,
3.5 miles, 3 hours, 500 feet elevation gain/loss (hike rating: strenuous).
Park HQ to trailhead 3 miles.

Few will disagree that the Alakai (lit., "to lead") Swamp is the most interesting and exciting place on the island. For interest, there is the beautiful mokihana berry — Kauai's flower — and the native rain forests; and for excitement, there is the swamp with its bogs, where a false step puts you knee-deep in mud and water. I recommend a lightweight, gore-tex or cloth hiking boot for this trail. You can bet on getting very wet and muddy.

A forest-reserve marker on Mohihi Road directs you to a spur road that goes to the trailhead. The swamp trail was built to supply a

Alakai Swamp Trail Boardwalk

pole line that was constructed during World War
II for Army communications. The first mile of the
trail is the width of a single lane road until it
reaches the Alakai-Pihea Trail junction. From
here, our trail follows a newly constructed (1998)
boardwalk that makes a steep decent to a small
stream, which eventually empties into Kawaikoi
Stream. Across the stream, the trail narrows and
makes a steep ascent.

Your nose may pickup the fragrance of the
mokihana (Pelea anisata) tree, which emits a
strong anise odor. It is a small tree whose small
berries are strung and worn in leis. Native to the
islands, the mokihana berry is frequently twined
with the maile vine to make a popular wedding lei.

The maile (Alyxia olivaeformis) vine is common along the trail, with its tiny, glossy leaves and tiny, white flowers. Unlike the Mokihana tree, the maile vine must be cut or its bark stripped before its musky, woodsy scent or anise is noticed.

After ascending and descending a number of small, fern-lined gulches, the broad, flat expanse of the swamp lies before you. A boardwalk has been placed over the muddiest places in the swamp to protect this environmentally fragile preserve. Be cautious or you'll find yourself ankle or knee deep in mud.

At Kilohana ("lookout point" or "superior") Lookout one has a magnificent view into Wainiha (lit., "unfriendly water") Valley, which extends from the sea to the base of Mt. Waialeale. Beyond Wainiha lies Hanalei (lit., "crescent bay") with its conspicuous wide, deep bay. It's an enchanting place to picnic, rest and reflect. If the cloud cover obstructs your view, just wait and it is likely to clear. Don't linger too long if the cloud cover remains. It can be very wet and very cold in the afternoon hours.

Kawaikoi Stream Trail,
1.75 miles, 1-1/2 hours
(hike rating: hardy family).
Park HQ to trailhead 3.8 miles.

Access to the Kawaikoi (lit., "the flowing water") Stream Trail is off the Mohihi (Camp 10) Road, which is passable only in a four-wheel-drive vehicle. The trail was made possible in 1975 when the Forest Service and the Hawaii

Chapter of the Sierra Club connected the Kawaikoi Trail with the Pihea Trail.

The route begins opposite a planted forest of Japanese sugi pines and follows the south side of Kawaikoi Stream along an easy, well-defined trail in heavy vegetation. During rainy periods, this is a muddy trail. A short distance past the 0.5-mile point, a trail sign indicates a place to cross the stream to join the Pihea Trail on the north side of the stream. If rocks are not visible, then the water is too high for safe crossing. The Kawaikoi Trail itself continues east on the south side of the stream to a point 100 yards past the 3/4-mile marker, where a trail sign marks the loop portion of the trail. During the 1-mile loop it is necessary to cross the stream twice.

In recent years, there has been a good deal of grass planting and herbicide work in the area in an effort to control blackberry, which is threatening to take over not only this area but also a number of other areas in the park.

There are many swimming holes in this generous stream and places along the bank to spend some peaceful moments. You may agree with Ralph Daehler, District Forester, Retired who says, "Kawaikoi is the most beautiful place on Kauai."

Poomau Canyon,
0.3 mile, 15 minutes (hike rating: hardy family). Park HQ to trailhead 4.5 miles.

About 0.5 mile past the trailhead for the Kawaikoi Stream Trail on the Mohihi (Camp 10)

Road is a marker identifying the Poomau (lit., "constant source") Canyon Trail. This short, easy trail passes through a small stand of Japanese sugi trees, enters a native rain forest, and ends overlooking Poomau Canyon, the largest and northernmost side canyon in Waimea Canyon. Across the canyon on the west rim, the high prominence is Puu Ka Pele (lit., "Pele's Hill") and Highway 550. Legend records that Pele, the fire goddess, left Kauai unable to find a suitable home. The caldera was created when Pele brought down her foot for the leap across the channel to Oahu. The caldera has since been filled with small stones some say by visitors as an offering to the goddess. The lookout is an excellent place for pictures of the canyon and for picnicking.

Kohua Ridge Trail,
 2.5 miles, 3 hours, 800 feet elevation gain/loss (hike rating: strenuous).
Park HQ to trailhead 5.5 miles.

The trailhead to the Kohua Ridge Trail (formerly the Maile Flat Trail) is off the Mohihi (Camp 10) Road, which is passable only in a four-wheel-drive vehicle. In 1988, the trail was cleaned and extended to Maile Flat for superb views of Waimea Canyon.

Originally constructed by the Civilian Conservation Corps, the Kohua Ridge Trail is a vigorous hike up Kohua Ridge to Maile Flat, which contains a heavy undergrowth of maile (Alyxia olivaeformis). A fragrant vine, maile has

glossy leaves, tiny white flowers and a musky,
woodsy scent of anise when it is cut or its bark is
stripped. Combined with mokihana berries, it is
a popular lei for weddings.

From the trailhead, the trail descends to cross
Mohihi Ditch and then swings left to cross
Mohihi Stream. If the water level in the stream
covers the boulders used to hop across, your hike
should end here. DO NOT cross if the water is
high. From the stream your trail follows a steep
and eroded path to the top of the ridge. Be alert
to side trails that hunters follow in search of feral
goats. The trail alternately ascends and descends
the ridge which is mostly heavily foliated with
koa and ohia trees. Periodic breaks permit a marvelous view deep into Koaie Canyon (left) and,
weather permitting, a view to the ocean.

The trail continues an up-and-down course
for the last mile. Look for pukiawe (Styphelia
tameiameiae) with tiny, evergreen-like leaves
with reddish-white berries. A sign at the end of
the trail means what it states. Beyond the sign,
"Kokua Trail Vista End," is a vertical drop into
Koaie Canyon. From here, a peaceful spot to
lunch, Poomau Canyon is north (right), Wahane
Valley is directly below and Koaie Canyon is
south (left). Only the view from the Awaawapuhi
Trail rivals this spectacular sight.

Mohihi Trail,
4 miles, 3 hours, 800 feet elevation gain/loss
(hike rating: difficult).
Park HQ to trailhead 6.2 miles.

I DO NOT recommend this trail because rain, a thick understory and side trails obscure your path to Koaie Camp. For me, the Pihea, Alakai Swamp and Kawaikoi Trails are safer and equally beautiful.

The first three miles of this trail were cleared several years ago, but since it receives few hikers, it can become quickly overgrown. If you choose to hike, DO NOT go beyond the cleared portion since the old trail is in disrepair as it cuts a circuitous route through the Alakai Swamp.

The trail begins at the end of the Mohihi (Camp 10) Road at a trail registry, crosses Mohihi Stream, skirts the upper part of the Koaie drainage, continues along a ridge top from which you'll have dramatic views and experience the beauty of the swamp.

Originally constructed by the Civilian Conservation Corps in the 1930's, the trail segment connecting the Mohihi-Waialae Trail and the Waialae Canyon Trail was destroyed by a hurricane in 1959. When funds become available, the trail will be repaired according to state officials.

Kaluapuhi Trail,
1.6 miles, 1 hour (hike rating: family).
Park HQ to trailhead 1.9 miles.

Kaluapuhi (lit., "the eel pit") is a favorite trail during plum season. It's a short,pleasant hike for the entire family with the prospect of finding plums along the trail.

The "Grand Canyon of the Pacific"

The first mile of the trail is wide and flat and essy to follow. At the 0.5-mile point, the trail to the left goes 0.5-mile to Route 550, 0.2-mile northeast of the Kalalau Lookout. The spur trail that goes straight leads to a grove of plum trees a short distance from the juction. If it is a good year for the delicious Methley plum, this trail will take you to some of the best trees. The pickings are generally good here because the only access to the trees is on foot.

Plum picking is regulated by the state. Picking rules change so check in at park headquarters or with Kokee Museum personnel for current regulations. Many local people bring the whole family and stay overnight to get an early start on opening day.

Pihea Trail,
3.7 miles, 3 hours, 500 feet elevation gain/loss
(hike rating: strenuous).
Park HQ to trailhead 3.8 miles.

Pihea ("din of voices crying, shouting, wail-
ing, lamentation") Trail begins at the end of the
Highway 550 at Puu o Kila (lit., "Kila's Hill")
overlooking Kalalau Valley. A hiking sign-in trail
registry identifies the trailhead. For your safety,
sign in and out in the registry.

The first 3/4-mile follows the remains of a
county road project which was begun in a cloud of
controversy and which terminated literally in the
mire when money ran out, along with the will-
ingness to continue. A road through the Alakai
Swamp and down the mountain to Hanalei

Pihea Trailhead

Kalalau Lookout - what a sight!

would have been a great tourist attraction and an engineering feat, but an ecological disaster.

From Kalalau lookout, you can usually see the white-tailed tropic bird (Phaethon lepturus) soaring along the cliffs of Kalalau Valley. This bird is white with large black wing patches above and 16-inch tail streamers. A similar bird that is all white except for red tail streamers is the red-tailed tropic bird (Phaethon rubricauda).

After enjoying the breathtaking views into Kalalau, your trail follows the rim of the valley to Pihea, the last overlook into Kalalau before the Alakai Swamp. From here, expect a wet, muddy trail through heavy vegetation. The trail makes an abrupt right turn as it enters the swamp and then drops in and out of a number of gulches to the junction with the Alakai Swamp Trail.

The Pihea Trail can be used as part of a loop trip from Kalalau into the Alakai Swamp, with a return to park headquarters via the Alakai

Swamp Trail or the Kawaikoi Stream Trail and the Camp 10 Road (see map).

Both the maile vine and the mokihana tree (see the Alakai Swamp Trail for description) are found along the trail and are favorites of both locals and visitors. The mokihana's powerful anise aroma attracts immediate attention.

Also common in this area is the ohia lehua (Metrosideros polymorpha), with its tufted red stamens that remind the visitor of the bottle-brush tree. A variety of tree ferns abound along the trail, the hapu'u (Cibotium chamissoi) and the amaumau (Sadleria cyatheoides) being most common. The latter grows to 10 feet. Its pinnate fronds were once used for huts and the juice from it for a reddish dye.

From the junction with the Alakai Swamp Trail, our trail continues over the newest portion passing through native forests, crossing small streams, and winding through verdant gulches until it joins the Kawaikoi Stream Trail.

Cliff Trail,
0.1 mile, 10 minutes (hike rating: family).
Park HQ to trailhead 2.1 miles.

The Cliff Trail provides a scenic vista of Waimea Canyon and a convenient departure point for the Canyon Trail. It begins after a short walk or drive down the Halemanu Road. Be quiet as you approach the lookout so that you do not frighten any goats that might be browsing there. Feral goats are commonly sighted here or walking along the pali area opposite the lookout.

Canyon Trail,
1.8 miles, 1 1/2 hrs, 500 feet elevation gain/loss
(hike rating: hardy family).
Park HQ to trailhead 2.1 miles.

The Canyon Trail is a popular hike. The trail
descends into a gulch and snakes along the cliff
to Kokee Stream and Waipoo (lit., "head water")
Falls, where you can picnic in the shade and
swim or splash in the stream. The best swimming hole is at the base of Waipoo Falls #1.

Although the Canyon Trail is steep in parts
and requires some stamina, it offers some of the
best views of Waimea Canyon. The trail begins
at the Halemanu Road and runs south along the
east rim of the canyon. It is somewhat precipitous in places, so be careful. At the Cliff Lookout,
which is 0.1 mile beyond the end of the
Halemanu Road, you get not only a view of the
canyon but also a view of the trail as it descends
and snakes along the cliff.

A common plant on the high, dry ridges is the
lantana (Lantana camara), which blossoms
almost continuously. Its flowers vary in color
from yellow to orange to pink or red; infrequently they are white with yellow centers. It is a low
shrub with a thick, strong wood.

A small, pretty, yellow-green bird, the aniani-
au (Loxops parva), is common in the high forests
of Kauai. In truth it is difficult for the less-than-
expert to tell the difference between the aniani-
au and the amakihi (Loxops virens), which is
the same size and yellow. However, if you get a
close look, the amakihi has a dark loral (space

between the eye and bill) mark that joins the eye and the curved dark bill. No matter, however, for they are both pretty birds.

From the falls, the trail makes a steep climb out of the gulch and ascends the pali, from which some of the best vistas of Waimea are had. Once again, be careful for while the trail is broad and easy to follow, at some places steep walls drop to the canyon below. There are numerous places to pause in some shade to enjoy the view through the canyon to the sea on the south side.

After a steep climb, the trail ends at Kumuwela Lookout, from where you can return on the Canyon Trail or connect with Kumuwela Road.

Black Pipe Trail,
0.5 mile, 1/2 hour (hiking rating: hardy family).
Park HQ to trailhead 2.5 miles.

This is a short spur trail that connects the Canyon Trail with the middle fork of the Halemanu Road. The trail descends into a small overgrown gulch and then climbs to follow the cliff to the Canyon Trail. It is along the pali that the rare and beautiful iliau (Wilkesia gymnoxiphium) grows. A relative to the rare silversword that grows on Maui, the iliau is endemic to Kauai and found only in the western mountains. It grows 4-12 feet high, it is unbranched, and the stems end in clumps of long, narrow leaves 6-16 inches long. Once in its life, the plant flowers in a flourish of hundreds of tiny yellow blossoms.

KOKEE TRAILS WEST

Nature Trail,
0.1 mile, 15 minutes (trail rating: family).
Behind Kokee Museum

This is a short, pleasant walk behind the museum in a forest of trees and plants common to the park. Before hiking, pickup a free copy of "Pocket Guide to Plants on the Nature Trail" in the museum.

Milolii Ridge Trail,
5 miles, 3 hours, 2,200 feet elevation gain/loss (hike rating: strenuous).
0.7 mile from Park HQ.

The trailhead is reached by driving south on Route 550 from park headquarters for one-half mile, turn right just past the 14-mile marker on Makaha Ridge Road and drive 0.2-mile to a junction. Milolii Ridge Road and the trailhead are on the right.

If you have hiked all of the trails in Waimea Canyon and Kokee State Park, then consider the Milolii (Lit., "fine twist") Ridge Trail. There is little to recommend the trail used primarily by goat and pig hunters. Indeed, you can drive the entire length in a four-wheel drive vehicle. At trail's end, the views do not compare to the Awaawapuhi or Nualolo Trails noted below.

Shade from tall koa and ohia trees is intermittent throughout the trail. Otherwise, it's usually a long, hot, dusty walk. Be alert for small, red strawberry guava trailside. When ripe, they are delicious. The trail, marked by conspicuous, white PVC pipe, makes a gentle descent before reaching several very steep, heavily rutted parts of the road that require some agility to negotiate, particularly when wet.

Just before the 2 1/2-mile marker, you have a view of the privately owned island of Niihau to the front-left. A trail shelter is on the right just past the marker. Niihau was purchased by the Sinclair Family in 1864. Today, about 200 Hawaiians live on the Island. Most work the cattle and sheep ranch much as their descendants did in the last century. Electricity has come to the ranch house and the school, but not to the homes of the residents. It's probably difficult for visitors to imagine life without television, telephones, shops or restaurants.

Located in a turnout under a canopy of trees, the trail shelter contains a picnic table and sufficient space to accommodate a tent. Sit quietly and you may be visited by the amakihi, a tiny, dull green-yellow, endemic forest bird. I watched several apapane, an endemic bird with a bright red crown, crimson breast and black legs and bill, foraging in the koa trees.

From the shelter the trail follows a steep, abrupt descent, one of several before reaching trail's end in a grove of koa and silk oak trees. Roads here go in different directions. Proceed cautiously north (right) a short distance to a view into Milolii Valley and the ocean beyond. A short walk south (left) leads to views of Makaha Valley. The microwave facility and numerous radio towers are in clear view on the ridge across the valley.

Nualolo Trail,

3.75 miles, 3 hours, 1,350 feet elevation
gain/loss (hike rating: strenuous).
50 yards west of Park HQ.

The Hawaii State Division of Forestry has
completed cleaning the Nualolo Trail and the
Nualolo Cliff Trail (see map) so that a marvelous 9-mile hike is possible by following the
Nualolo-Cliff-Awaawapuhi trails.

The Nualolo Trail starts between the ranger
station and the housekeeping cabins in Kokee,
and if you follow the suggested 9-mile hike, you
will exit the Awaawapuhi Trail on Highway 550,
1.5 miles from Park Headquarters.

The first part of the trail passes through a
native forest of koa trees with their crescent-
shaped leaves for a pleasant, cool hike. After an
initial ascent of about 300 feet, the trail then
descends about 1500 feet to a number of view-
points overlooking Nualolo Valley. The first 1.5
miles of trail are broad, posted and easy to follow. A variety of ferns, the beautiful kahili ginger, and edible passion fruit, thimbleberries and
blackberries are found along the trail.

The trail narrows somewhat at the 1.5-mile
marker, but then opens again at the 2.25-mile
post. After this point, you're certain to see the
rare, endemic iliau plant (see Black Pipe Trail
for description). You may also find ripe strawberry guava, a small, red golf ball-sized fruit.

There are several steep parts on the trail in
the last mile so be cautious. At the 3.4-mile
marker, the Cliff Trail goes right for 2.1 miles

until it reaches the Awaawapuhi Trail and the
Nualolo Trail goes straight to numerous vista
points about 2800 feet above the valley. Trail's
end is a marvelous place to picnic and to enjoy
the solitude. If you walk out to the end of the
ridge, you will have a view of the Na Pali Coast
to the north (right) and the beach fronting
Kalalau Valley.

Nualolo Cliff Trail,
2.1 miles, 1 1/2 hours (hike rating: strenuous).
Reached via Nualolo or Awaawapuhi Trail.

If you have reached the Nualolo Cliff Trail
junction from the Awaawapuhi or Nualolo Trail,
you should hike the Cliff Trail for the views into
Awaawapuhi and Nualolo valleys are outstanding. Additionally, you're likely to see feral goats
here as well as the rare, delicately beautiful
Kauai hibiscus.

From the Nualolo Trail, the Nualolo Cliff
Trail is mostly level until just before reaching
the Awaawapuhi Trail, where it makes an easy
ascent. One-fourth-mile markers identify the
way along which you are certain to see goats
foraging for food and bounding on the steep
slopes in the upper valley. The trail was cut to
provide hikers with a crossover trail between
two marvelous trails and to offer some of the
best views of the Na Pali Coast.

At the 1.5-mile point, the trail emerges on a
flat area used by campers. Here, the trail is not
clearly marked. Hike up the ridge away from

the valley lookout and you will locate the trail and shortly, a white PVC-pipe-marker.

Between the 0.5 and 0.25-mile markers, look for the rare, endemic Kauai hibiscus (Saint johnianus) with its small, delicate, orange blossom. It's a find.

After an easy uphill, the Nualolo Cliff Trail joins the Awaawapuhi Trail where you can go 0.3 miles left to the end of the trail or go 2.8 miles right to Kokee Road.

Awaawapuhi Trail,
3.25 miles, 2 1/2 hrs, 1,600 ft. elevation gain/loss (hike rating: strenuous).
Park HQ to trailhead 1.5 miles.

Awaawapuhi Trailhead

The Hawaii State Division of Forestry has completed cutting, brushing, posting and taping the Nualolo Trail and the Nualolo Cliff Trail (see map) so that a marvelous 9-mile hike is possible by following the Awaawapuhi-Cliff-Nualolo Trails. I would begin such a trek on the Nualolo Trail and end traversing the Awaawapuhi Trail since the latter is a more gradual ascent.

The Division of Forestry has a guide "Awa'awa'puhi Botanical Trail Guide," which is available from the forestry office in Lihue (see Appendix) and from the Kokee Museum. The Division of Forestry has identified and posted with white PVC pipe 58 plants found along the trail. The white pipe with numbers on top identify the plants while the pipes with numbers on the side are mile markers. Learning about these native and introduced plants will add a dimension to your experience.

Of the trails that extend to points high above the Na Pali Coast and the extraordinarily beautiful valleys of the north shore, this is the best. You should be in good condition before attempting this hike and be prepared with water and food. The rewards are great as you pass through tropical forests to view the extremely precipitous and verdant valleys of Awaawapuhi (lit., "ginger valley") and Nualolo.

The trail begins at a large, open parking area northwest (left) off Highway 550 about halfway between the Kokee Museum and the Kalalau lookout. There is a forestry trail marker at the trailhead. The trail is well-maintained, and mileage markers show the way.

The first part of the trail passes through a moist native forest, dominated by koa trees, for a pleasant, cool hike. Koa trees grow to a height of more than 50 feet. The koa has a light gray bark that is smooth on young trees and considerably furrowed on mature trees. The leaves are smooth, stiff and crescent-shaped. Often called Hawaiian mahogany, the wood is red with wavy grain that makes it popular for use in furniture, woodwork and ukuleles. In older times it had nobler purposes, having been used for war canoes, surfboards and calabashes. A variety of ferns, the beautiful kahili ginger, and edible passion fruit, thimbleberries and blackberries are also found along the trail.

The trail then descends gradually through a moist native forest which becomes drier scrub as it reaches the ridges above the valley. You are most likely to see feral goats in the pali area. With binoculars you can watch goats forage while you pause on any one of a number of lookouts about 2500 feet above the valley. Additionally, you will probably sight helicopters flying tourists in, out, and over the pali, since the Na Pali Coast is a favorite for those who are unable or unwilling to make the trip on foot.

Just before reaching the 3-mile marker, a white PVC-pipe post identifies the Cliff Trail that goes south (left) 2.1-miles to the Nualolo Trail, which leads to the main road between the ranger's house and the housekeeping cabins.

The Awaawapuhi Trail continues for 0.3 mile from the junction to a vertical perch above the Na Pali Coast. This is the best place to lunch and to watch for goats while enjoying enchanting views into Nualolo and Awaawapuhi valleys. It's a startling and exciting place.

Appendix

Division of State Parks
State Building
3060 Eiwa St, Room 306
Lihue, HI. 96766
✆ (808) 274-3444

1. Camping permits
   for state parks and
   Kalalau Trail.
2. Hiking information.

Division of Forestry
State Building
3060 Eiwa St, Room 306
Waimea Canyon
Lihue, HI. 96766
✆ (808) 274-3433

1. Hiking information.
2. Camping premits for

Kokee Ventures
P.O. Box 819
Waimea, HI 96796
✆ (808) 335-6061

1. Kokee cabin
   information
   and reservations.

Department of Parks
and Recreation
County of Kauai
4444 Rice St, #150
Lihue, HI. 96766
✆ (808) 241-6670

1. Camping permits
   for county parks.

Pedal & Paddle
Ching Young Village
Hanalei, HI 96714
✆ (808) 826-9069

1. Complete line of
   camping & backpacking
   equipment; sales
   and rentals.

Kauai Bus
✆ (808) 241-6410

1. Schedules and
   information.

Captain Zodiac
✆ (808) 826-9371

1. Ferry to Kalalau
   Valley.

Index

TRAIL NOTES

TRAIL NOTES

TRAIL NOTES

TRAIL NOTES

TRAIL NOTES

TRAIL NOTES

TRAIL NOTES

TRAIL NOTES

TRAIL NOTES

TRAIL NOTES

Our new video:
"Hawaii On Foot"
See Hawaii as few have with

Robert Smith

For his video, **HAWAII ON FOOT**, Smith has taken from his books some of the best dayhikes and backpacks on the four major islands to give the viewer a sampling of the best trails on Maui, Hawaii, Oahu and Kauai.

Here are hikes in Haleakala and Hawaii Volcanoes National Parks, backpacks deep into the Kauai wilderness, strolls into Maui's verdant valleys and walks along the black sand beaches of Hawaii.

There are hikes for the dayhiker and the backpacker, for the novice and the experienced outdoorsperson and for children and their grandparents.

HAWAII ON FOOT also contains camping and state rental housekeeping cabin information – Hawaii's best bargain – and tips on hiking and backpacking equipment.

ORDER FORM

HIKING KAUAI $11.95

HIKING MAUI $11.95

HIKING HAWAII $10.95

**HAWAII'S BEST
HIKING TRAILS** $15.95

***VIDEO:* HAWAII
ON FOOT** (special) $10.95

FORWARD TO:

NAME:_____

ADDRESS:_____

CITY_____STATE:_____ZIP:_____

QUANTITY		PRICE	TOTAL
HIKING KAUAI	@	$11.95	=
HIKING MAUI	@	$11.95	=
HIKING HAWAII	@	$10.95	=
HAWAII'S BEST HIKING TRAILS	@	$15.95	=
***VIDEO*: HAWAII ON FOOT** (special)	@	$10.95	=
	Postage/Handling (1st Class)		= $3.95
	TOTAL ENCLOSED		=

MAIL TO:
Hawaiian Outdoor Adventures Publications
34 Kaui Place, Kula, Maui, HI 96790

ORDER ONLINE: http://www.maui.net/~hionfoot